ISLAM AND THE ARAB INVASION

DR. NICHOLAS F. PAPANICOLAOU

ISLAM AND THE ARAB INVASION
by Dr. Nicholas F. Papanicolaou

Printed in the United States of America.

ISBN 9781498493314

www.xulonpress.com

As the deglobalization movement expands worldwide, as evidenced by Brexit, Islam will be its principle casualty. National cultures will reassert themselves over the imported Arab-centric culture that Islam represents.

Dr. Nicholas F. Papanicolaou

DEDICATION

This book is dedicated, with respect and love, to those Christian martyrs who have been killed, usually in the most appalling manner, by ISIS and other jihadi representatives of the Global Islamic Movement. In particular, it is dedicated to Bishop Francois Murad, who was reportedly decapitated with a kitchen knife by the Syrian "resistance" in 2013. His crime, like many others similarly beheaded, was that he was a Christian.

ACKNOWLEDGMENT

I wish to thank my Editor, Deb Williams, for putting up with me and, once again, being an effective helper in getting this new book ready. I enjoy working with her, and her unfailing enthusiasm is contagious.

There are photographs in this book that bear witness to my involvement as one of three Co-Founders with the World Public Forum "Dialogue of Civilizations," with various national Orders of Merit of the nations of Spain, Ukraine, Portugal, Sweden, and with the Sovereign Order of Saint John of Jerusalem, Knights of Malta, The Ecumenical Order (TM, Malta 2001 and 2009). I wish to make clear that the views I express in this book are exclusively my own and are not in any way associated with or representative of the above organizations or Orders of Merit.

I also thank my publishers, Xulon Press, for their support with this book.

Dr. Nicholas F. Papanicolaou

TABLE OF CONTENTS

Part Three: The Limits on Freedom of Speech and Freedom of Religion in the United States

Part Four: Toward a Grand Strategy

Part Five: Some Conclusions

FOREWORD

Some will see the title of this book and immediately think it is written by someone who has an irrational fear of Islam.

I do not.

I have a rational fear of Islam.

I have studied its history and its Arab-based culture code over the fourteen centuries it has existed. I know its cruelty to the "kuffar" or infidel. I know of its harems, its sated lifestyle, its cultural retrogression and abuse of women, its Janissary Corps that abducted able-bodied Christian boys and turned them into barbaric executioners of Christians, and its brutal laws. I know that Allah is principally referred to as The Lawgiver, the propagator of hard laws, but not of loving others. And I do not see in it the message of loving our neighbor as ourselves, the message of not doing unto others what we do not wish done unto us, which both Christianity and Judaism teach.

I was born in Greece, a country that for fourteen centuries has had to spill the blood of its people in order to defend its Christianity, its language, and its culture from Arab-centric Islam.

But Greece is also the country that produced Alexander the Great, a king still very much revered in what is now the Muslim world, from

Egypt, to the Middle East, to Central Asia, and Iran. On the fields of Opis, close to Babylon, Alexander gave a speech in the year 324 BC to nine thousand representatives of all the different people and religions in his vast kingdom. Known as "The Oath of Alexander" the speech established the ties of friendship between those peoples and Greece. A part of his speech said:

"From now on, let all mortals live as one people, in fellowship, for the good of all… See God (you will notice he refers to one God, not the twelve Olympian gods) not as an autocratic despot, but as the common father of all and thus your conduct will be like the lives of brothers within the same family" (parenthesis is mine).

The ties of friendship between Greek, Egyptian, Middle Eastern, and Asian transcend and predate, by at least a thousand years, the advent of Islam. Islam has interfered with and disrupted that friendship, though the friendship survives to this day.

Arab-centric Islam aggressively came into countries that had civilizations that were superior to its own and destroyed them. It brought nothing new to most nations and in fact retrogressed many. Egypt, for example, had established from the Third Dynasty that commenced in 2,778 BC, religion and laws that are admirable to this day. The theology of Ra, the great god, had established that living according to the Will of Ra meant practicing justice and charity. So justice and charity are not concepts original to Islamic thought. There were also Egyptian laws on wills, equal inheritance rights for men and women, labor contracts, and lease contracts. There was no penalty of death in the Egypt of 3,000 BC, let alone a penalty for the chopping off of limbs as punishment for stealing.

As a Greek, I am an heir to Alexander and the friendship with Middle Eastern, Central Asian, and North African peoples. I am what they have for more than two thousand four hundred years called, with evident friendship and admiration, a "Yunani"—which means an "Ionian"—a Greek.

Islam presents itself as a "Civilization Alternative." The Muslim Brotherhood says so, as do the writings of many Islamic scholars through the centuries. Does that mean that the civilizations Islam sought to obliterate were, or are, worthless? Civilizations and cultures like the Sumerian, Persian, Hittite, Babylonian, Assyrian, Indian, Afghan, Lydian, Greek, Egyptian, Phoenician, and even the Mongolian, Uighur, Indonesian, and Filipino—were they all worthless compared to the Arab-Islamic culture? None of these countries were Arab, but they have wound up with Arab customs and culture: inter-marriage between first cousins, cruel punishment for minor crimes and tribalism; all brought into their societies under the banner of Islam. Truly, are they happy with that? Happy with their civilizations being taken over by a theretofore inferior culture emanating, not from culturally prominent Egypt, or spirit-elevating Greece, or Rome, but from the life-extinguishing deserts of Arabia?

I will cite here some examples of the imported culture that Islam is. Persia (modern-day Iran) has a grand ancient history, beginning with Cyrus the Great around 560 BC. Cyrus, and his successors on the throne, Darius, Xerxes, and Artaxerxes established a tradition of friendship and, in fact, admiration for the Jews, whose land they had conquered. The Old Testament is full of stories of the special rights given to the Jews, including the story of Daniel (who Cyrus instructed his people to revere after he threw Daniel into the lions' den in 539 BC and he survived without a scratch), to Xerxes and his Jewish wife Esther, to Artaxerxes giving the right in 445 BC to Nehemiah (a Jew) to rebuild the walls of Jerusalem. Then Islam came to Persia, turned it against its own ancient history, and made it a mortal enemy of the Jews. But the hatred shown by the Ayatollahs toward Israel and the Jews is totally alien to Persian culture. Do we see evidence here of Arab prejudices taking over a non-Arab country?

Let us cite here some further examples of how Islam forcefully altered the character of the people of nations it conquered and turned them against their own selves and their own history. Ethiopia is the modern-day heir of the ancient kingdom of Sheba. King Solomon of Israel, who ruled around 980 BC, had very friendly relations with the kingdom of Sheba, as did subsequent kings of the Israelites. Yet Ethiopia is today predominantly Muslim and very belligerent toward Israel and Jews. Yemen is another example. In fact, in the 6th century AD, King Dhu Nuwas of Yemen converted his entire kingdom to one state religion, Judaism. This was done a few decades before the advent of Islam to Yemen. But today Yemenis profess to hate Jews and Judaism, thus contradicting their own historical traditions and past.

Likewise, before the advent of Islam, there were many Arab tribes that were Jewish or Christian. As we have seen, even Mohammed's first wife was Christian. So, if Mohammed lived the perfect life to be copied by all his followers (as the Sunnah teach in Islam), then should not all Muslims be blessed when they marry and respect Christians, as Mohammed respected his first wife?

As to Arab Jewish tribes (a term which today sounds completely paradoxical), Dr. Saleh Al-Jallad in his book *Pedagogy of Arab Governance* tells us that they were concentrated mainly in Medina, Yathrib, and northwest Arabia. They, too, were turned against their culture and traditions by the onslaught of Islam. Entire kingdoms in Arabia, such as the kingdom of Edessa ruled by King Abgar VIII (177-212 AD) had converted to Christianity. They were the kingdoms mostly of the advanced south Arabian Peninsula. Then Islam came out of the desert peoples, known as "the A'arab," which Dr. Al-Jallad tells us means people of "a totally different, degraded, and relatively uncivilized way of life," and forced them into its fold. Could it be that A'arab desert tribalism and its prejudice toward the "outsider" metastasized into Islam's hatred of the non-Muslim? Dr. Al-Jallad characteristically tells us about the Arab tribe that "all intra-relationship is subordinate to the tribe, and the tribe is based inherently on blood relationship. It is the tribe who fends off the enemy…" Did this tribalist mindframe extend itself onto Islam and, through Islam, into all Muslim nations and their enmity toward non-Muslims?

By the way, we must note here that according to Dr. Al-Jallad's accurate definition of the "A'arab" as the desert people, modern-day Egyptians and Middle Easterners are not A'arabs. I think this is the inescapable conclusion from his history. And it is corroborated by the simple fact that ancient Egypt was not A'arab, nor was its estimable civilization. I doubt very much that the Pharaohs from 3,000 BC all the way to the dynasty of Greek Pharaohs (the Ptolemids) who reigned to about 60 BC thought of themselves, or the people they reigned over, as A'arabs. Similarly, aren't modern-day Tunisians the genetic descendants of the ancient Carthaginians, and not the descendants of the A'arab?

Can any of the learned men from Islam please enlighten us as to exactly at what point in time it is claimed that the descendants of the Pharaoh Ramses and Tutankhamen, and ancient Egypt's population, changed genetically and became A'arab? Suffice it to say that today when I look at modern-day Egyptians or Lebanese, I do not see A'arab genetics, but the genes of ancient Egypt and of the ancient Phoenicians (who lived on the coast of what is now Lebanon). They have no connection to the A'arab who were the people of the desert.

Do we see here, yet again, how Arab-centric Islam has come into other peoples and civilizations and has sought to confuse and convince them with the fiction that they are Arab?

What has happened to the cosmopolitan Persians of old, who accepted all other cultures into the kingdom of Cyrus the Great? What happened to the learned Egyptians of old, who would share their considerable knowledge with other nations like Greece?

Have all these illustrious civilizations of old been sacrificed forever at the altar of Arab-centric Islam? And if Arab-centric Islam is to shove off our planet all these illustrious civilizations, what is its own claim to fame? What great contribution to the betterment of mankind does Arab culture claim? As we shall see later in this book, even its claim that it invented Algebra is wrong. Simple Algebra was invented by the ancient Babylonians around 1900 BC and then perfected by the ancient Egyptians and the Greeks (Pythagoras and others). A simple Google search on Algebra proves this.

So, with the advent of Islam to many nations that were civilizationally much more advanced than desert Arabia, what really happened? Dr. Al-Jallad actually speaks on page 40 of his book of "the colonization of Europe by the 8th century Arabs." So there it is: the colonization of not only Europe, but of the world, through Islam. What right can Arab-centric Islam really claim to obliterate, and consider itself superior to, those ancient civilizations? Was it perhaps the principle known as "might is right" and nothing more? Was it just the curved Arab scimitar, designed to cut off more body parts in one fell swoop, and nothing more? And we are now called to bend our knee to this culture?

As a civilized person, as a Christian, as a historian, as a child of God, and as an heir to Abraham, Isaac, and Jacob, not to mention Alexander the Great, I protest this invasion of the world.

Christianity, Judaism, Buddhism, and Hinduism, to mention other principal religions, do not present themselves as "civilization alternatives." They respected the civilization of the countries they came into. They focused on spiritual teaching only. Greece, for example, did not lose its ancient civilization, its artists, its philosophers, and its historians with the advent of Christianity. It kept its culture but accepted the God of Abraham, Isaac, and Jacob. What a difference we see here between how Christianity came to ancient civilizations and charmed them with its love, and how Islam came to similar civilizations with its air of (questionable) superiority, its violence, and its negation of anything but itself.

Christianity brought with it the message of love, which originates in ancient Judaism. It also brought forgiveness of sins, through confessing them and turning away from them. It did not bring in a super-imposed Arabic code of justice, or a message of conquest and destruction of the infidel. And it brought with it a gentle message of seeking God, which it shares with Judaism.

Abrahamic religions, which Islam claims to be one of, also bring with them certain strictures, certain commands. Since Islam accepts the Old Testament in its theology as a God-given book, perhaps more attention ought to be paid to what the Old Testament says in Genesis 12:3. God is speaking to Abraham, giving him a promise that He blesses his offspring from the child of His promise, Isaac. And then God says to Abraham: "I will bless those who bless you, and I will curse him who curses you." In fighting against and killing Christians, who are all children of the promise of God to Abraham and Isaac, Muslims are disobeying a direct command of God. They are cursing Isaac's offspring and will be cursed themselves. God's Word is not to be ignored. They cannot believe in their theology that the Old Testament is God-given and then contradict it, and expect that there will not be punishment.

I feel a great sympathy for those in Islam who, like me, are God-seekers. We are all on a quest to find God, to get closer to Him, to feel His love for us. Some pursue God through Islam, perhaps because that is how they were raised and that is all they know. I was free to pursue God any way I wished. I have found the love of Jesus. That does not make me a criminal.

I do not hate Muslims for their approach to finding God. Equally, they must not hate me for my approach to finding God. Our ways are different but we are still brothers just as Alexander, and Jesus, asked us to be.

So, can we learn to co-exist in peace, each in his own pursuit of God, or must we yet again spill precious blood? And if we do, what will God really think of us?

If we are all God's creation, imagine how our Creator feels seeing us kill each other in His name. What pain we must cause Him, fighting in His name! He must feel like a Father whose children are killing each other in His name. What true Father likes to see that?

So can we live and let live?

If some really are wrong in their method of pursuing God, let them find out on their own through whatever revelation God gives them.

Human judgment of others, accompanied by coercion and cruelty, really are not necessary. Let God's love envelop all those whom He chooses to give His love to. They will feel and know His love as He blesses them with it. Others will not, and thereby should know they are on the wrong track.

INTRODUCTION

Since the dissolution of the Ottoman Empire and of the Caliphate in 1915, the forces of Islam have been quiescent as never before. The Christian world has never had such a period of peace since the founding of Islam by Mohammed in 622 AD. That is when he left Mecca under threat to his life and began the Hijra, his pilgrimage to spread Islam throughout the world. Until 1915 AD, the forces of Islam have been a constant threat to the very existence of Western civilization and the Judeo-Christian moral code that underpin it. Indeed, the history of Arab cruelty and violence unleashed on the Christian nations after the death of Mohammed in 632 AD has no equal in history. People who had already been Christian for centuries in lands such as Egypt, Sudan, Libya, Tunisia, the entire Middle East, Yemen, what is today the United Arab Emirates, and Saudi Arabia were forcibly converted to Islam or killed. The historical evidence of a strong Christian presence in these countries is overwhelming: from the enormous Christian cathedral in Sana'a (capital of Yemen) which was completed around 570 AD to evidence of early Christian colonies that thrived in the seventh century AD on the island of Sir Bani Yas (in modern-day Abu Dhabi), to the monastery of Sinai, we have evidence of flourishing Christianity that was tragically extinguished by the onslaught of the enslaving and plundering Arab armies of Islam. Indeed, it offends righteousness itself to hear the modern-day apologists for Islam claim that Islam must re-conquer "the native lands of Islam," forgetting that those "native lands" were once thriving Christian communities. Indeed, the only truly "native" lands of Islam are Mecca and Medina.

The record of this cruelty and violence continued uninterrupted until 1915 AD. Landmarks of the violence through the centuries include the attack on France and the Battle of Tours in 732 AD that saved Paris, the repeated attacks by the Arab armies of Islam on Constantinople starting in 717 AD, the conquest of Andalusia in 711 AD, the conquest of Malta, Sicily, Sardinia, Brindisi, Bari, Taranto, Provence (all accomplished prior to 880 AD), the initial Christian response with the First Crusade in 1095 AD, the fall of Constantinople in 1453 AD, the naval Battle of Lepanto in 1571 AD, the repeated attacks against Christian Russia and Armenia, the Armenian genocide in 1915-1917, and the massacre of two hundred thousand Greek Christians in Smyrna in 1922. Indeed, to this very day the evidence of the intent of Islam to conquer and subdue the Judeo-Christian world is both irrefutable and depressing.

The violence only stopped for a brief period after the Ottoman Empire and Caliphate collapsed in 1915 AD. But with the advent of untold riches that oil exports brought to the Muslim world in the Arabian Peninsula and Iran beginning with the first oil shock in 1973, Islam resumed its march against the Christian world. The Israeli "occupation" of lands on the West Bank that have been in Jewish hands since around 1400 BC has provided the excuse with which to fire Islam's dreams of renewed conquest and world dominion.

Some may wonder if what I say is Islamophobia. Being Greek, I reserve for myself the right interpretation of the word "phobia."

In Greek it means a condition of fear, but not "unreasonable fear." Apologists for Islam seek to make it look like Islamophobia is an unreasonable, if not neurotic, fear of Islam. The correct answer to their misinformation is to say that all one needs to do is study what Islam has done for fourteen hundred years to have a justified fear of it.

We can only understand what Islam is if we understand the historical context of what Islam has already been and what it aspires to be again. Otherwise, we are doomed to see history and violence against the Christian world repeat themselves.

This book will explore how in our present time the forces of "civilization jihad" working from within are far more dangerous than the forces of violent jihad, also known as "radical Islam," "violent extremism," or any other euphemism our political leadership invents in order to placate us into a sense of false security.

We will begin in Part One with a review of where Islam is today in various Western countries, with a special focus on America. We will discuss how Islam uses Western liberal laws on freedom of religion and freedom of speech with which to bring down our civilization and culture. In Part Two we will discuss how our existing laws are being violated, as our political leaders blithely stand by and even allow themselves to become mouthpieces for the conqueror, usually in the fatal pursuit of a few more votes from the domestic Muslim population. We will remind our readers of those laws, and how they should now be immediately enforced to stop the dissolution of our liberal civilization. In Part Three of this book we will look back to historical and legal precedents established by the Western democracies to oppose and defeat similar challenges. Such past challenges include internal espionage and sedition within the United States, the confrontation and eventual defeat of internal communism in America, as well as earlier legal limits we placed on freedom of religion and freedom of speech to prevent problematic religious teachings from corrupting our Judeo-Christian civilization and values. In Part Four we will look at some essential actions that Western countries, and in particular the United States, can take that are short of war and could preserve the peace. Lastly, in Part Five we will offer some conclusions on the findings of this book, and what needs to be done.

A concluding remark: the content of this book is not written in anger at Muslims. As Christians, we are called to love them. And we do. We pray that they will come to accept the Lord and to know His love. We pray that they will see God, the God of Abraham and Isaac and Jacob, not as the strict and relentless lawgiver that Allah personifies, but as the loving and forgiving God who is full of grace and promises restoration and restitution. But, at the end of the day, they are entitled to their religion and values, as we are entitled to ours. The trouble begins when they insist, as they invariably do through whatever means available, on imposing their religion and Arab-inspired laws in our countries and on our Judeo-Christian way of life. Islam is at war with the rest of the world. Unlike what various pundits think, war is a one-sided state of affairs. Dialogue requires two participants. War only requires one. The sooner the whole world comes to realize that Islam is at war with it, the less blood will be shed.

It is my hope that this book will both inform and caution all who read it as to what the dangers are and where we are presently headed. There is still hope of avoiding mass bloodshed if the Western world insists with its laws and law-enforcement on preserving what has been built in the West over the centuries with the shedding of so much Christian blood. My fervent hope is that there will also be reform within Islam, the kind of reform that Egypt's President al-Sisi called for on his New Year's Day address in 2015 to the Islamic scholars at Al-Azhar University in Cairo. Al-Azhar is generally considered to be the foremost university on Islamic theology in the world. The kind of reform President al-Sisi was calling for was a cry of hope that Islam would stop its aggressive ways and finally understand the principle of "live and let live."

Not all Muslim countries are alike. The version of Islam practiced in Indonesia is far more lenient and accepting of others than the Islam practiced in Saudi Arabia, Afghanistan, or Pakistan. The reason is that in Indonesia, the Koran and Sharia law are not fully observed and practiced. If Islam could at least reform itself upon the Indonesian model, the world would be a far safer place for all.

Until that day comes, Christianity, Israel, and the West have no alternative but to defend themselves, drawing on their past for the application of laws already conceived and enacted, to safeguard their civilization.

In closing, let me remark that there is no such thing as "freedom to destroy freedom." And there is no "freedom of religion with which to destroy religion." These are principles Western democracies must re-discover and re-embrace in order to assure their survival. The latitude of the West's freedom of religion and freedom of speech laws must be adjusted, as it has been in the past, in order to oppose the one religion that presently uses our freedoms for the purpose of conquering us.

President Reagan famously said that freedom is never more than one generation away from being lost. Each generation must do its duty to protect and preserve its freedom; otherwise ever-present challenges will destroy it. Rhode Island was set up in 1636 by refugees led by Roger Williams, who fled the Massachusetts Bay Colony because they wanted more freedom of worship. The land Williams and his group occupied was purchased from Indians. It had nothing to do with Great Britain. They were free from imperialism. And yet, within eight years, through fear and disunity with the other Puritan settlements in New England, Rhode Island subjected itself to the British Crown and submitted to a royal charter. Rhode Island, like the other New England towns and settlements, had to fight the War of Independence one hundred and fifty years later in order to free themselves from the yoke of royal rule they allowed themselves to come under. Freedom is never more than a generation away from being lost. Much blood and suffering then is required to regain it. Let's not lose ours to Islam.

Islam calls itself "a civilization alternative." It is a "whole-life system" and not just a religion. It represents an existential challenge to our freedoms. What does "civilization alternative" mean? It really means destroying Western democratic civilization, our Judeo-Christian values, and replacing them with an Arab-centric Islam and the Global Islamic State. All this is made clear in the Muslim Brotherhood's "An Explanatory Memorandum" written on May 22, 1991, which was introduced into evidence by the U.S. Government the Fall of 2008 in U.S. Federal Court in Dallas during the trial of the Holy Land Foundation, a Hamas charity front operating in the U.S. Holy Land Foundation was found guilty of raising $12 million in the U.S. that was then turned over to Hamas, a terrorist organization. Its conviction was upheld in the Federal Appeal Court.

Dr. Nicholas F. Papanicolaou
2016

PART ONE

ISLAM AND THE WEST, FROM ITS ORIGINS TO TODAY

Chapter 1

A BRIEF HISTORICAL REVIEW

The relationship between Islam and the Western and Christian world has always been strained. Rare and short periods of accommodation have been replaced with long periods of strife and extreme violence.

Mohammed began his conquests within the Arabian Peninsula from the year 622 AD, when he escaped from Mecca under threat of assassination. The merchant class of Mecca despised him because his new religious teaching threatened, inter alia, the commercial and souvenir business they had set up centered on tourists visiting the meteorite known as the Ka'aba. The preaching of a new god, Allah, seriously detracted from the worship of the meteorite.

Until Mohammed's time, Christians, Jews, and pagans had lived in Mecca more or less in peace with each other. In fact, Mohammed's first wife was a Christian. She was a wealthy widow, older in age than Mohammed. She provided the financial stability for Mohammed, who began to preach his new religion in the year 612 AD.

Between the years 622 AD and 632 AD when Mohammed died, many battles were fought by his burgeoning army against other Arab tribes, with the aim of consolidating his power. His followers increased from the grand total of fifty-five people when he left Mecca, to hundreds of thousands by the time of his death.

In 624 AD, the first of these battles was fought, the Battle of Badr. A much smaller army from Medina, led by Mohammed, defeated a large army from Mecca. Mohammed immediately invoked Allah as the reason for his victory. He used the victory as proof of Allah's blessing upon him and his message. This victory established a fundamental principle that we will observe in Islam: the only proof of Allah's blessing, the only miracle in its hagiography, is victory on the battlefield. Unlike Christianity and the many eyewitness testimonies of miracles performed by Jesus and the apostles, even to this day, Islam offers no evidence or even mention of eyewitness miracles in its theology. In Islam the living god does not manifest himself on this earth to show his power and approval, except for victory on the battlefield. This is why, to this day, battlefield victory is the only confirmation of approval by Allah of what his followers do. Also, in Islam Allah can change his opinion or laws, as the Islamic principle of abrogation teaches. Thus, with a god who may change his laws, Islam does not offer the reliable constancy of an unchanging God and unchanging principles that Judaism and Christianity offer. We can rely upon the unchanging nature and laws of God, but can a Muslim?

Having preached the principle of Allah's approval through victory on the battlefield against overwhelming odds, however, Mohammed immediately ran into trouble at the next great battle, the Battle of Uhud, on March 23, 625 AD. His army from Medina was again outnumbered by the Meccan army. In the initial stages of battle, the Muslims (Meccans) gained the upper hand. But Mohammed's archers broke formation and charged headlong for the Meccans' supply camp, which lay unprotected. The lure of all this easy plunder was overwhelming.

This gave the opportunity to the Meccan cavalry to charge into the gap in the Muslim lines. The cavalry quickly decimated the Muslim army. Mohammed himself was seriously wounded.

When, after the Meccans withdrew, the leaders of the Muslims came to Mohammed anxious to know why Allah had withdrawn his approval, he enunciated the principle that Allah does not approve of plunder. They had lost the battle because they had sought to steal and plunder, instead of doing Allah's work. Islamic practice after Mohammed's death, however, runs contrary to this principle. As Islamic hordes attacked city after city in the Christian world, the terms Islam's forces would offer the Christians would be immediate surrender with submission to Islam, or three straight days of rape, plunder, and death. How this subsequent practice can be reconciled with Mohammed's teaching after the Battle of Uhud remains unanswered. But it does help us understand why Mohammed also preached the principle of "progressive revelation" (see Sura 5:48) under which revelation received later prevails over revelation received earlier wherever there is any contradiction.

An equally important fact is that the Koran was not written contemporaneously with when Mohammed received his revelations (from the Archangel Gabriel as he claimed). All the pieces of paper on which his followers had scribbled these revelations (Mohammed was illiterate, so he did not write these down himself) were allegedly collected by the third Caliph, Othman (or Osman), and first put into one book in 650-653 AD. At the Battle of Yamama in December 632 AD, just after Mohammed had died, a great number of Mohammed's eyewitness friends and close associates had been killed. This was one of the first battles fought by the new Caliph, Abu Bakr, to keep control of the Arab tribes that were attempting to leave Islam after Mohammed's death, known as "the Apostate Wars." So, the third Caliph, Osman, decided that it was urgent to save the testimony of the surviving eyewitness associates of Mohammed, and so decided to put together the Koran and the Hadith (the sayings of Mohammed) that his surviving associates could testify to. Please remember here, again, that there were no eyewitness accounts to any miracles performed by Mohammed or by Allah.

It is impossible to track if what was put into the Koran (as we know it today) was original (i.e. from Mohammed), or not. In Islamic history we are told that Osman collected and destroyed by fire any versions of the Koran that did not agree with what he had put together. Thus, academic experts cannot establish the present-day Koran's originality because the only evidence that exists is certain scraps of eighth-century Korans and not the whole book of verses. And those scraps are in Muslim hands and not made available to Western scholars to study. As to the experts on the Islamic side, they have effectively not been able to prove the originality of these documents. To put this in clearer language: there is no genuine academic evaluation that has taken place with open availability to historic evidence, open discourse, and openness to differing points of view. Eminent Western experts in Islamic studies, like Christoph Luxenberg, have been limited in simply analyzing the graphics of early versions of the Koran. What they have reasonably established so far is that the earliest versions of the Koran do not include diacritical markings, i.e. dots or marks over a word that can radically change its meaning. Diacritical marks were added to much later versions of the Koran, and when those versions of the Koran are studied by Western experts, they tell us that many sentences with the "added" diacritical markings just do not make any sense. We do know for a fact, however, that verses in the Koran on some particular subjects do not match other Islamic verses written, for example, on the walls of very early mosques and also on coins of early Muslim kingdoms. This is a crucial issue for Muslims because the Koran is supposed to be "the perfect word of Allah." As such it is not subject to changes or re-interpretations.

Robert Spencer in his book, *Did Muhammad Exist?* (ISI Books, USA, 2012), points out one such substantial difference between the Koran as we know it today and the inscriptions that appear in the Dome of the Rock mosque in Jerusalem (completed in 691 AD). He points out that Sura 19:33 reads in the Koran as follows: "Peace be upon me, the day I was born, and the day I die, and the day I am raised alive."

But the inscription appearing in the Dome of the Rock mosque reads: "Peace be in HIM the day HE was born, and the day HE dies and the day He shall be raised alive!" (Caps are mine.)

If the Koran is the perfect, unalterable word of Allah, how could anyone dare change his words and put different words on the walls of the mosque?

Interestingly also, notwithstanding Islam's present-day persecution of the cross of Christianity, coins minted in the 7th century in lands that the forces of Islam had already conquered, bear Mohammed's name and the cross. For example, in the 640s and 650s coins minted in Palestine, which had been conquered by the Arab armies of Islam in 638 AD, bear the inscription "Mohammed" and show a figure holding a cross. These coins are problematic to Islam for two reasons: first because they bear an image of Mohammed, which is strictly forbidden in Islamic theology, and second because they show him holding a cross. These coins are authenticated and undeniable. Likewise, during the Caliphate of Yazid (680-683 AD) coins that have also been authenticated depict Yazid and feature a cross. And in the earlier Caliphate of Muawiya (661-680 AD) coins depict him holding the cross with a crescent over it. The bathhouse in Palestine was completed and dedicated in 662 AD, with an official inscription that mentions Muawiya and bears the cross.

How then can modern-day Islam's hatred of the cross be reconciled with the use of the cross in early Islamic kingdoms? Were they using the cross then to appropriate to themselves the legitimacy of the cross and to lull their newly conquered people into a false sense of security? But if this is what they were doing, how does that reconcile with the command in the Koran not to take Christians and Jews, or their religion, as friends and instead to hunt them down? The evidence we have from these coins of an Islamic kingdom using the cross as a symbol of the kingdom is completely antithetical to the perfect word of God represented in the Koran. Confusing, isn't it?

Let us now turn our attention back to the Koran. It is important to know which chapters (Suras) of the Koran were written last, because they prevail over the previous ones. Mohammed himself preached the principle of "progressive revelation." This principle states that because he himself was receiving revelation in stages, whatever he said later overruled whatever he may have said earlier, if there was a contradiction. There are many such contradictions in the Koran. I will give here just one example: Sura 41:7 teaches that when a martyr for Allah dies he goes to heaven (Jinnah) with his wife or wives. Yet Suras 52:20, 37:48, 56:22, 56:36, and 78:33, plus Hadith (the eyewitness sayings of Mohammed) Salih Bukhari 4:54:476, 6:60:402 and 4:55:544 say it differently: they teach that when a martyr goes to heaven, he will have the seventy-two "houris"—the perpetual virgins—there to amuse him. And eminent Islamic theologians like al-Suyuti who died in 1505 AD further represent paradise in completely sensual terms of sexual pleasure for the "elected." He states that: "Each time we sleep with a houri (one of the seventy-two virgins) we find her a virgin. Besides, the penis of the elected never softens. The erection is eternal." So which is true? That the martyr goes to heaven with his wife, or that he goes to heaven to enjoy the seventy-two virgins? And if the latter, what does his wife do? Watch while he enjoys himself, or does she simply not count? Well, Islamic theology teaches the following about women in paradise: "A woman will have only one husband in paradise, and she will be satisfied with him. (Shakh 'Abd-Allah ibn Jibreen; see also Fatwa No. 11419).

But here is an important question for the would-be martyrs for Islam: what if the teaching on the seventy-two virgins is wrong, for whatever reason? What if it is seventy-two delicious grapes (as some prominent Islamic theologians are now teaching) and not seventy-two virgins? Will it then have been worth all the hateful killing of others? What if upon arriving at the gates of heaven they find that they are condemned for their crimes against their fellow human beings? Is it not far better to have lived a life of love and of compassion for their fellow humans, and not an imam-induced life of hate and cruelty to others?

In my earlier book, *Islam vs. The United States* (Oak Leaves Publishing, USA, 2011), I supplied in Appendix 1 a list of the Suras from the Koran, showing the true chronological order (according to Islamic scholars themselves) in which they were revealed to Mohammed. It is noteworthy that Sura 5 and Sura 9 are, chronologically, the 112th and 113th chapters of the Koran's 114 chapters. They therefore are of particular significance to Muslims because what they teach overrules any earlier principle in Islam. By the way, since this book was published in 2011, the level of awakening in America to the true nature of Islam has been rising steadily. The American public has gone from a non-existent understanding of Islam to a great awareness of its brutality, thanks to the repelling acts of Islamic terrorism and to informative books on Islam.

Let us look into some of the verses from Sura 5 and 9. We discover that they command the forcible conversion, mutilation, or death of the unbelievers, as well as commanding that Allah's laws (the Sharia) must be imposed on the world. Here are some examples:

Sura 5:33: "Indeed the penalty for those who wage war against Allah and His Messenger and strive upon earth (to cause) corruption is none but that they be killed or crucified or that their hands and feet be cut off from opposite sides or that they be exiled from the land. This is for them a disgrace in this world; and for them in the Hereafter is a great punishment." (Saheeh International)

So here we have the principle of brutal murder or mutilation of the unbelievers (Jews and Christians) or, at best, the exile from their homeland so that Muslims can take them over with full religious justification. It is this religious justification that propels Muslims to this day to say that all "native" lands of Islam must be returned to Islam. Such lands would of course include Andalusia and Grenada in Spain, all of Provence in France, all of Greece, Malta, Sicily, Sardinia, Brindisi, Taranto and Bari in Italy, and even what is today Romania, Hungary, parts of Austria, Israel, Jerusalem, etc. Indeed, in the eyes of a practicing Muslim, these lands are presently soiled by the infidel (the kuffars) living there. It is of no importance to Islam that these lands were once solidly Christian, including other countries, which were once solidly Christian and now are under Islam such as Egypt, Sudan, Libya, Tunisia, all of the Middle East, Turkey, etc. It is also of no importance to a practicing Muslim that these lands were conquered in brutal ways by the forces of Islam and that, within the scope of human history, Islam represents but a small era of fourteen hundred years within the historically documented story of humanity that spans five thousand years at least.

Sura 5:49 (Al-Maida): "You shall rule (or "judge") among them in accordance with God's revelations to you. If they turn away, then know that God wills to punish them for some of their sins. Indeed, many people are wicked." Note: "al-Maida" (the title of this Sura) means "the Feast."

Here we have twin principles that are very problematic to Jews and Christians. First the concept that Muslims are taught that their destiny is to rule over us, and second that this rule will be in accordance with God's revelation given to them, i.e. the Koran and Sharia law instead of our Constitution. Does reading this explain why every practicing Muslim wishes to replace the U.S. Constitution with Sharia? The Constitution is man-made law, while Sharia is Allah-decried law.

Sura 9:29: "Fight those who do not believe in Allah or in the Last Day and who do not consider unlawful what Allah and His Messenger have made unlawful and who do not adopt the religion of truth from those who were given the Scripture (i.e. Jews and Christians). (Fight) until they give the jizzya (the tax to be paid by the infidels to the Muslim authorities) with willing submission and feel themselves subdued." (parenthesis mine) (Saheeh International)

Sura 8:12: "I will strike terror in the hearts of those who disbelieve. Therefore strike off their heads and strike off every fingertip of them."

The only obligation imposed on Muslims before they resort to violence against the infidel is the "Dawa"—the call or invitation to join Islam. Sura 17:15 says: "We do not punish until We send a messenger." The messenger is to invite the infidels to join Islam and pay the "jizzya"—the submission tax. In *Al-Hidaya, A Classical Manual of Hanafi Law*, the "Rules of Warfare" specify "that the Prophet did not commence combat with a people without first inviting them to Islam." Since Mohammed was the perfect example of a man, everything he did (recounted in the Sunnah, and everything he said outside the Koran (recounted in the Hadith) is an example to be followed. Characteristically, former President Ahmadinejad of Iran issued a Dawa to the United States in

May 2006. If the Dawa is not immediately accepted, it amounts to a declaration of war in the mind of a Muslim. That is exactly where the United States is today, the uninformed protestations of President Obama and Secretary Kerry notwithstanding.

By the way, Islam's fury is directed at the infidel, even if he or she is a member of the immediate family. A mainstream commentary to the Koran, authored by one of their great scholars, ibn Kathir, to Sura 5:28 praises Muslims who kill their own relatives if they do not follow Allah and his Prophet. Thus, the first Caliph, Abu Bakr, tried to kill his own son for not being Muslim. Omar, the second Caliph, slaughtered his relatives for the same reason. According to ibn Kathir, Allah was greatly pleased in these two for their acts of faith and granted them entry into Jinnah.

Any echoes of present-day Islamic violence here?

Does all this remind us of what ISIS is doing to the "infidels" today?

This is the "Religion of Peace"?

Does the New Testament teach such things?

Does modern-day Judaism teach such things?

Or Buddhism, or Hinduism?

Do we see that it is Islam that is the problem and not "radical Islam"?

Do we understand that there is no separate book of "radical Islam"? That there is only one book of Islam, the Koran, and its spiritual child Sharia law?

Such then were, and still are, the religious teachings and principles that propelled the armies of Islam on an unprecedented blood bath against Christians, beginning in the year 632 AD. The first Caliph, Abu Bakr, who was a former foe of Mohammed's from the Mecca merchant class, began the conquests outside the Arabian peninsula. He was followed by an even bloodier Caliph, Omar, who in short order conquered what is now Iran, the Middle East, Jerusalem (in 638 AD), Sudan, Egypt, Yemen, and other countries. The Arab forces of Islam did not arrive in those countries as liberators. Overwhelmingly, they arrived as vicious conquerors, killers, rapists, and thieves, who used their religion to justify their crimes.

Patriarch Sophronius of Jerusalem, whose sorry destiny it was to surrender Jerusalem to the Caliph Omar, wrote extensively on what it was like to live under Islamic rule. Contrary to the perpetual apologists for Islam who say that it has been benevolent on the infidels it conquered if they submitted and paid the jizzya, Sophronius paints a picture of constant fear and of Christians locked up in their homes by fear. In one of his writings he says:

"As once with the Philistines, so now the army of the godless Saracens has captured the divine Bethlehem and bars our passage there, threatening slaughter and destruction if we leave this holy city (he means Jerusalem) and dare to approach our beloved Bethlehem." (Sophronius, Christmas Sermon, 506, quoted in Hyland, Seeing Islam).

NOTE: at the time the names "Muslim" and "Islam" were unknown to the West. The invading armies were called "Saracens." The whole concept of Islam, i.e. submission, was a later name adopted by Muslims. At the time, they were simply viewed by Christians as "Saracens," which means conquerors and murderers. They had not yet wrapped themselves in the claimed sanctity of submission to a lawgiver God, named Allah.

These are the historical facts.

By the year 880 AD, the armies of Islam had turned the Mediterranean into a Muslim lake. They controlled both the southern and the northern coasts of the Mediterranean Sea.

This military feat was accomplished by the union between the merchant class of Mecca, the various Arab tribes, and Mohammed's base in Medina. To accomplish peace with the merchants of Mecca, Mohammed allowed certain of their customs to be accepted into Islam. Some of our readers may have noted that devout Muslims show each other a hand sign, the Shahada. The right hand is raised with the index finger standing up, and the thumb and middle finger folded at the base of the index finger. This symbolizes that there in only one god, his name is Allah, and his prophet is Mohammed. This is the signal that every ISIS fighter gives to another. But if there is only God to be worshipped, why do Muslim pilgrims still worship the Kaaba, the meteorite in Mecca that dates to pre-Mohammed days? Each pilgrim must go and touch the glass behind which sits the Kaaba. How did this custom creep in to Islam? It did because Mohammed needed to make peace with the merchant class of Mecca, who depended on selling souvenirs and trinkets to tourists coming to see the meteorite. So, it was incorporated into official Islam. An object is therefore worshipped that has little to do with the theological concept of the Shahada (one God). Indeed. Is there a teaching in Islam that says that Allah or Mohammed touched the meteorite or taught that it was somehow instrumental in the theology of Islam?

Parenthetically, we must mention here that in August 2014 President Obama attended in Washington, D.C. the meeting of the U.S.-African Leaders Conference. After the group photograph with all the African Presidents, most of whom are Muslim and a few of whom are Christian, President Obama very clearly gave one and all the Shahada salute.

in Obama flashes the Muslim *shahada* to delegates of the US-African Leaders Conference in Washington DC in August 2014.

Press took this astonishing photo as the African dignitaries joined Obama, who hosted tate Department auditorium for a group photograph. It was published in an article in Mail, and it was the only use ever of the photo.

display is the distinctive Muslim gang sign: The index finger points straight up while the derneath and presses against the digital phalange of the middle finger. The remaining ezed against the palm in order to highlight the extended forefinger. The extended finger ne one-God concept of Muhammad and is understood by all believers to be a symbolic uslim affirmation of faith: There is but one God and Muhammad is his messenger.

evers stick their index finger in the air, they demonstrate they are partisans of od concept. And they also affirm their belief in Muhammad's claim he was the n God and man. They also demonstrate they are part of the *umma*, the exclusive tribe of believers that Muhammad started 1,400 years ago.

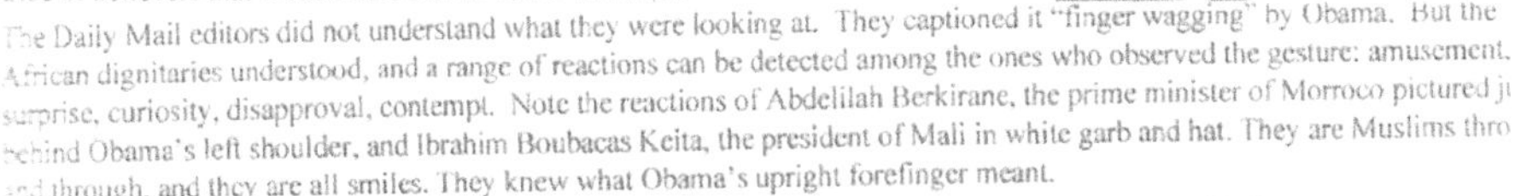

The Daily Mail editors did not understand what they were looking at. They captioned it "finger wagging" by Obama. But the African dignitaries understood, and a range of reactions can be detected among the ones who observed the gesture: amusement, surprise, curiosity, disapproval, contempt. Note the reactions of Abdelilah Berkirane, the prime minister of Morroco pictured ju behind Obama's left shoulder, and Ibrahim Boubacas Keita, the president of Mali in white garb and hat. They are Muslims thro and through, and they are all smiles. They knew what Obama's upright forefinger meant.

Let us also note that one of Islam's main objections to Christianity is the Christian belief in the Trinity—Father, Son, and Holy Spirit. The objection is because Islam believes that Allah is not part of anything and does not share his power or glory or worship with anyone or anything. So how does the Kaaba fit in to this theology?

As to the Christian theology of the Trinity, here are excerpts from the Koran. Sura 5:75 states: "The Messiah, son of Mary, is no more than a messenger like the messengers before him, and his mother is a saint." And Sura 5:73: "Pagans indeed are those who say that God is a third of a trinity."

So Jesus is not God, He is not part of the Godhead worshipped by Christians, because there can only be one god, and his name is Allah. So how does worshipping a meteorite fit into this?

Armed with the religious justification provided by Islam, Muslim armies laid siege to Constantinople in 717 AD, almost conquered Paris in 732 AD, conquered Constantinople in 1453 AD, conquered and held Budapest for almost 200 years, and laid siege to Vienna as late as 1683 AD. Then with the rise of technology in the West, the Christian states became more powerful and began a series of military victories against the forces of Islam. These victories, commencing with the Naval Battle of Lepanto in 1571 AD, had an enormously dispiriting effect on Muslims. The miracles they needed, the only miracles in Islam, on the battlefield were no longer forthcoming. The forces of Allah were being defeated, so the Christian God must be stronger. The Ottoman Empire, now based in Constantinople (renamed Istanbul by the Turks) remained as the center of the Caliphate. The Sultan combined in his person both the secular emperor and the Caliph, or spiritual leader and heir of the Prophet.

The combination of the West's technological innovations and its consequent wealth slowly ate away at the Ottoman Empire until it collapsed in 1915 AD. Now the last vestige of Islamic power was gone. The Muslim world went quiescent. Allah no longer performed miracles for them. The last fatwa (religious order) of the Caliphate was issued by Sheikh Shawish on March 10, 1915. It called for the re-conquest of Islam's "native lands." And then the armies of Islam were extinguished until 1973 when the tremendous oil wealth brought about by the oil shock began to be viewed again in the Muslim world as the new miracle.

Allowing such a "miracle" to give violence-prone courage to Muslims is a big mistake for America and the West. America no longer needs the energy resources of the Middle East. It has enough coal, natural gas, and oil to be completely self-sufficient. It is because of the Green Lobby that we are not energy self-sufficient and continue to import oil, thus placing enormous funds in the hands of Islamic regimes. Has anyone attempted to put all this on a ledger? National security and not aiding our enemies on the one hand, and green policies on another to see which way the scales lean? Has there been any informed national dialogue on this issue? The answer is no. The Democrat Party and most of the Republicans are under the control of the Green Lobby. In the meantime domestic jobs in energy are lost, our trade balance suffers, and billions of our dollars go into the hands of our most rabid enemies. It is madness.

Since 1973, we have been living in a world of a resurgent Islam. Political leaders in the West have miserably failed to recognize this. Political correctness has lead them to believe that Islam can be dealt with in civil ways like other political groups, and that in the meantime it must be treated as a "protected class" along with homosexuals and other classes that may be discriminated against. Such a view is suicidal blindness as the mounting evidence of what the forces of Islam are doing to Europe, and now to the United States, demonstrates. Indeed, the European homeland is already altered, pulled away from its Judeo-Christian foundations and dragged through the streets on its way to the jizzya (submission tax).

When I think of Islam, I receive caution and guidance from the words of a devout Muslim, Tamil Ansari, who authored a book titled *Destiny Disrupted*. I highly recommend it. At the end of the chapter that he devotes to the history of early Islam, up to the death of Ali, the fourth Caliph, he states: "After Ali, Islam became just an empire." The implication is that any sincere religious feeling or approach that some of its founders had was now gone. Islam was now just a secular power, an empire. Ali was killed by a poisoned sword in 661 AD, while praying at a mosque in Kufa. His assassin was a Sunni, a follower of the Mecca group who had also attempted to kill Mohammed. With his assassination, the claim of spiritualism in Islam was gone. Thus sayeth the Islamic historian, Tamil Ansari.

Chapter 2

MUSLIM IMMIGRATION TO EUROPE

At the end of World War II, a number of countries in Europe desperately needed to rebuild their ravaged homeland. The competition with Soviet communism was also in urgent mode, as it was recognized that if European economies did not build up fast enough, those countries would fall easy prey to the siren song of communism. There was also another problem: insufficient manpower. Beginning with Germany, whose male population had been decimated by the war, and going on down the list of participants in the war, many countries had urgent manpower shortages. The authors of the German economic miracle had a solution. It was to encourage labor migration from Turkey, and to a lesser extent from other southern European countries like Greece. The result was the "gastarbeiten" (guest worker) program. What the German authorities did not take stock of was that they were now importing large numbers of Muslim immigrants. As is almost always the case with new government programs, they are dressed up under false guises in order to gain initial public acceptance.

The gastarbeiten program in Germany was presented under the guise that these guest workers were not acquiring permanent residence status, let alone citizenship. They could be deported at any time if their employment was terminated. This, however, is not how the program developed. Once in Germany, the Muslim immigrants took advantage of German laws to remain in the country. Very few of the guest workers from other European countries like Greece remained. They went home as their local economies improved, but not so with the immigrants from Muslim countries. In addition to Germany, France, Belgium, and the Netherlands needed extra manpower. For reasons associated with their particular colonial histories, these countries wound up importing Muslim workers from their former colonies: Algeria, Tunis, and Morocco in the case of France, Pakistan in the case of the United Kingdom, Libya in the case of Italy, African countries like the Congo in the case of Belgium, and Indonesian Muslims in the case of the Netherlands.

According to the Pew Research Center, here are the Muslim population numbers for Europe (excluding Turkey—if indeed it can be considered European), as well as the percentages of Muslims compared to the rest of the population:

Year	Muslim Population	As % of Total in Europe	
1990	30,000,000	4.1%	
2010	44,000,000	6.0%	
2030	58,000,000	8.0%	(projected)*
2050	71,000,000	10.0%	(projected)*

*Note: the above does not take account of the more than 1.5 million Muslim immigrants that came into Europe during 2015. The figures for 2010 include 10 million Muslims living in Russia. Source: Pew Research Center Muslim Population Estimates

Russia has the largest number of Muslims among European nations numerically. However, it is not bound by the oftentimes insidious laws of the EU. It manages its Muslim population far better than the West. There are lessons to be learned from its paradigm. President Putin made a speech to the Russian Federation's Federal Migration Service in January 2012, and said:

"On the whole the adaptation of guest workers is a separate, and comprehensive issue. We must create the conditions for immigrants to normally integrate into our society, learn Russian and,of course, respect our culture and traditions and abide byRussian law. In this regard, I believe that the decision to make learning the Russian language compulsory and administer exams is well grounded. To do so, we will need to carry out major organizational work and introduce corresponding legislative amendments. I'd like to ask the Federal Migration Service and other departments to submit specific proposals to the government. These proposals should be openly discussed with ethnic minorities as well as public and religious organizations.This should be mandatory for all guest workers regardless of their future employment."

What lies between the lines here?

First, these new regulations are mandatory for guest workers, and in Russia "mandatory" means mandatory. Second, the Russian Orthodox Church must approve any such regulations, evidently not leaving elbowroom for Muslims to seize ground. Let's remember that Russia has for centuries been a bitter enemy of Islam, having suffered at the hands of first the Muslim Tatars and then the Ottomans since the 12th century. We need look no further than the cupolas of Russian cathedrals, which show the Christian cross piercing the Islamic half moon lying at the cross's feet, to know what the historic Russian attitudes toward Islam are.

Московского Кремля

Examples of Russian church cupolas, showing the Holy Cross piercing the half moon of Islam.

Now back to western Europe: equally alarming as our statistics on the Muslim population growth in Europe is the fact that, according to the Pew Research Center, the native European population's median age is eight years more than the Muslim immigrant population, forty years for native Europeans as opposed to thirty-two years for Muslims. Lastly, and alarmingly, the median age of Christians in Europe is forty-two years old, i.e. the Christian population's median age is ten years older than the Muslim immigrant population.

Other developing European countries followed the German lead, with Italy, France, Switzerland, and the United Kingdom coming easily to mind. The justification for this was economic development. Little thought was given by Europe's political leaders to the religious and cultural problems that they were to encounter down the line. No comparative studies were done in any of these countries to analyze which country or countries were best suited as a source of imported labor. In a conversation I had with Walter Schwimmer, an Austrian politician who rose to be Secretary General of the Council of Europe (which unlike the twenty-eight member European Union, includes all European countries), he could not recall that any such analysis had taken place. Former colonial powers just turned to their colonies for cheap labor. When I mentioned to him that in Buenos Aires, Argentina in the 1980s there were long lines outside the Italian Embassy of Italo-Argentine immigrants who were pleading to get their Italian passports back so they could re-emigrate back to Italy and that the Italian authorities would not issue them, but rather the Italian government continued to import immigrants from Libya and other Muslim countries, Mr. Schwimmer was surprised. So, the question remains and is a valid one: why did the political leadership not better analyze its guest laborer needs? Why were Italo-Argentines (the sons of Italians who had emigrated to Argentina) or other workers from Latin America (Mexico included) not better candidates to be invited into fellow Christian countries in Europe, instead of the culturally alien and religion-alien Muslims from North Africa and the Middle East? Why?

Europe is now certainly paying the price, as the failure of "multi-culturalism" becomes painfully obvious.

And then came the landmark year of 2015. For years illegal immigration, many times hiding under the political refugee banner, has inundated Europe. The principal entry paths into Europe have been from Libya and Tunisia into Italy, and from Turkey into Greece. The deterioration and humanitarian crisis, which developed in Syria, provided useful cover for uncontrolled immigration. While the Obama Administration sat on its thumbs and allowed this to happen, hundreds of thousands of people in Syria, including a substantial percentage of Christians, were allowed to be caught in the crossfire. Turkey, ever tuned on how to profit from possible opportunity, turned human smuggling into a national industry. "Refugees" from Iraq, Afghanistan, Pakistan, and other countries were easily allowed to cross into Turkey's southern border. It defies imagination to think that the Turkish government could not better guard this border, especially since this is their common border with the Kurds in northern Iraq, and the Turks are always keenly vigilant of any movement across that border. So their border was willingly opened to a new market: "refugees." Instant tourism. The "refugees" were sold everything from food, to water, to transport, to even the inflatable boats and life jackets they would need to cross from Turkey into Greece's Aegean islands, the first European Union country. In the summer of 2015 more than 1.5 million people came into Greece this way. On arrival at the shore of a Greek island, they would slash their inflatable boats to assure that they would not easily be sent back. Then they would appear before one of the EU documentation centers to be identified as refugees from Syria. Typically they would appear with no form of identification. No background checks, no past history. Greek police would discover in the countryside caches of passports jettisoned by these "refugees" from Afghanistan, Iraq, Pakistan, and other Muslim countries that had nothing to do with the humanitarian crisis in Syria. This is how one of the murderers who participated in the Paris massacre of one hundred thirty people on November 15, 2015 came into Europe. He was identified by Greek police as having come into the country as a "refugee" on October 3, 2015. As a further example, in November 2015 five "students" were arrested in Honduras holding fake Greek passports (see Op-Ed page of *The Miami Herald*, November 23, 2015.) They were all jihadis, on their way to the United Sates.

While Greece was struggling with this tidal wave, Germany's Chancellor Angela Merkel made the command decision to announce that Germany would take up to one million of these people. This put on turbo boost the human smuggling ring operating in Turkey. On the Aegean island of Kos alone, more than one thousand "refugees" were arriving each day in the summer of 2015 from Turkey. The Greek authorities were swamped. And Europe was being placed on an even faster track to loss of identity and of its Judeo-Christian character. What a betrayal of Europe's people by their globalizing leaders! Is it any wonder that the British people opted for exit from the European Union and its overarching bureaucracy?

How did the European Union respond, with considerable prodding from Germany's Chancellor, to this invasion? On March 18, 2016 an EU—Turkey Action Plan was agreed upon and signed by Turkish

Prime Minister Davutoglu and the President of the EU. Here are its main points of agreement:

1) Turkey will accept back from Greece all "irregular" refugees who reach Greece after March 20, 2016.
2) For every refugee being returned to Turkey from Greece, the EU will accept another refugee from those already in Turkey (alleged to be 3.3 million).
3) Turkey will now take all necessary steps to prevent new sea or land routes for "irregular" refugees.
4) Once the flow of these "irregular" refugees was been slowed down or stopped, a Voluntary Humanitarian Admission Scheme will be activated.
5) By the end of June 2016, all necessary steps will be taken to lift the visa requirements for Turkish citizens traveling to the EU.
6) The EU will deliver to Turkey the initial 3 billion euro allocation under the Facility for Refugees in Turkey, to be followed by a further 3 billion euros by the end of 2018.
7) Upgrade the present Customs Union between the EU and Turkey.
8) The accession process for Turkey to become a member of the EU will be "re-energized."
9) The EU and Turkey will work together to improve humanitarian conditions inside Syria.

Do we see anything wrong with this treaty?

a) Turkey now receives a 6 billion euro reward for having turned illegal refugee crossings of its country into a national, and very profitable, industry.
b) Turkey now gets to legally send up to 3.3 million "regular refugees" into the EU, to replace every "irregular" refugee who is

returned to it from Greece. So now 3.3 million new residents of Muslim background will come into the EU, all handpicked by the Erdogan government. By the way, does anyone think that there was, at least, a fact-finding committee from the EU who went to Turkey to substantiate the claim that there presently 3.3 million refugees in Turkey?

c) Turkish citizens now get to travel in the EU with no visas.
d) The accession negotiations for Turkey to join the EU are to be "re-energized" so that one day Turkey may gain entry into the EU and further flood it with its Muslim citizens.

All this good faith from the EU is extended to Turkey and its Islamic President, Recep Erdogan, who has reportedly jailed more than sixty thousand people including journalists, diplomats, Armed Forces officers, teachers, and government employees after the failed coup on July 15, 2016. The same Erdogan who after winning an election as Prime Minister of Turkey some ten years ago, was asked by a journalist how he reconciles democracy (a man-made system) with Islam (God's law). His answer famously was: "Democracy is like a bus. You ride it until you get to where you want to go." True to that principle, is it not interesting that since the July 15, 2016 coup attempt by the military, Mr. Erdogan has placed more than sixty thousand people under arrest spanning university professors, government officials, military officers, and even doctors and lawyers? In fact, he ordered the release of thirty-eight thousand convicts from Turkey's jails in order to make room for his political opponents. Democracy may well be breathing its last breath in Turkey right now. The secular Muslim state that Condoleezza Rice always held up as an example of a modern secular Muslim democracy is crumbling. Once again, our high officials failed to really reckon what they are dealing with. Erdogan could not have survived the coup of July 15 unless Islamist masses were behind him. It was they who came out into the streets, died (some two hundred sixty of them), and withstood the military's last-ditch effort to save the secular state set up by Kemal Ataturk in the wake of the fall of the Ottoman Empire.

So now the EU is relying on Turkey and its leader, President Erdogan, to decide who will be the 3.3 million new "regular refugees" who get to go to the EU legally. Could this be the final straw that will bring Europe down, an invading army of 3.3 million "regular" refugees?

Nations are like individual people. They have a past, good or bad.

What is the true, historical, character of Turkey? When it was still called the Ottoman Empire, it brutally subjugated millions of people. After its conquest of Constantinople and most of Greece in 1453 AD, it turned the Greeks (as it did other Christians) into third-class citizens. First in their empire came the Muslim Turks, then Muslims of other nations that had subjugated, and last came the Christians, the "Dhimmis" or "Giaurs," as the Turks called these lesser forms of human life. Their legal rights were curtailed, as was the right to teach the Christian faith as well as the Greek language and culture. These were kept alive among the Greeks only through the existence of the "secret schools" that operated at night. It was through these secret schools that for the four hundred years of Muslim occupation of Greece, Christianity and the Greek language were preserved. Greek priests taught at the secret schools. The penalty, if they were discovered by the Ottoman authorities, was hideous death. The prescribed punishment often was skinning the priest alive or roasting him over burning coals. Among the Greeks, priests were honored for this reason. If a priest who taught at a secret school managed to die a natural death, the family would, after his death, change their surname to the priest's first name and add "Papa" (which in Greek means "priest") at the beginning of the new name. Thus the progeny of Father Nicholas would become known as "Papanicolaou" in honor of the risks the priest had taken. The proliferation of Greek names, which begin with "Papa", is evidence of the role priests played in preserving Christianity and the Greek language and culture during those four hundred dark years.

There is one further fact that needs to be mentioned here on the subject of Turkey. In all of Scripture, there is only one spot where the place that Satan has his throne on earth is identified. This reference can be found in Revelation 2:12-13. In the passage on the Letters to the Church of Pergamum:

Then to the angel (messenger) of the assembly (church)in Pergamum write: "These are the words of Him Whohas and wields the sharp two-edged sword: 'I know where you live—a place where Satan sits enthroned.

'"Yet you are clinging to and holding fast My Name, and you did not deny My faith, even in the days of Antipas, My witness, my faithful one, who was killed in your midst—where Satan dwells.'"

Here the Lord is commending His church in Pergamum, in spite of the fact that He identifies (twice in the same paragraph) that this is where Satan has his throne on earth.

So, where is Pergamum? It is in modern-day Turkey, close to the ancient city of Troy. Satan has his throne in Turkey. Be very leery of what comes out of Turkey.

One more interesting fact. In August 2016, after Erdogan put down the coup attempt, a Parliamentary delegation from Turkey came to Washington to demand the extradition to Turkey of a Turkish imam, Gulen, whom Erdogan considered responsible for the July 15 coup.

The delegation had the usual tour of meetings with U.S. Congressional leaders and the Obama Administration. Then whom else did they spend substantial time with? The Council on American Islamic Relations and its nationwide Executive Director, Nihad Awad. What role does CAIR play for Erdogan's Turkey? Awad came out with a very complimentary statement about Turkey, just as Turkey's secular regime established by Kemal Ataturk in 1919 is being destroyed and replaced by an Islamist regime. But CAIR is a 501c3 not-for-profit organization. Is it supposed to be participating in politics, supporting the Erdogan government? Should CAIR be obliged to now register as a lobbyist for the Turkish government? We shall see.

On September 29, 2016 President Erdogan of Turkey announced that Turkey no longer recognizes the 1923 Treaty of Lausanne, which ended the Balkan Wars between Greece and Turkey and ceded almost all the islands in the Aegean Sea to Greece. Could it be that one reason he is taking this position is that as a devout Muslim he considers these islands part of the "native lands" of Islam?

What is the historical background of these islands? They were all Greek from ancient times, and have had Greeks and Greek-speaking populations from at least the 10th century BC. They include Patmos, where the Apostle John wrote Revelation, Delos, which was the treasury and sanctuary of the Athenian Alliance in the 5th century BC, Milos where the famous Aphrodite of Milos (presently at the Louvre Museum) was discovered, Samos where the philosopher Pythagoras was born, Kos where Hippocrates the father of medicine was born, Rhodes where the Christian Knights of Saint John of Jerusalem were based and defended Christianity from 1302 AD to 1522 AD, etc. etc. Those islands came under the Ottoman yoke for about two hundred years beginning in the 15th century AD, and yet Mr. Erdogan and his fellow Islamists consider them Turkish and Muslim ground. How long will it be before Islamists like Mr. Erdogan bring us to war again with their preposterous claims? Do we see how it important it is to constantly be vigilant, to constantly stand against Islamic claims lest our hard-won freedoms be consigned to oblivion?

England now has 3.2 million Muslims. Germany 4.8 million (prior to the extra immigrants that came in in 2015), France 4.7 million, Italy 2.2 million, Spain and the Netherlands 1 million each. How do these countries intend to deal with their own declining birthrates, rising Muslim birthrates, and the failure of these immigrants to assimilate by accepting the values and culture of their host countries?

In a recent survey done by the Pew Research Center ("Five Facts About the Muslim Population in Europe") negative views of Muslims in Europe are overwhelming. Here is the data:

Country	Percentage of Population With Negative Views of Muslims*
Hungary	72%
Italy	69%
Poland	66%
Greece	65%
Spain	50%
Netherlands	35%
Sweden	35%
France	29%
Germany	29%
UK	28%

Note: this survey was conducted before the 2015 New Year's Eve rape and sexual assault incidents on one thousand women in the cities of Cologne, Frankfurt, and Hamburg.

Now let us turn our attention briefly to the aftermath of the 1.5 million "refugee" immigration that flooded Europe in 2015. The *New York Times*, that bastion of liberal-progressive values, reported in its October 31, 2015 issue in an article written by Andrew Higgins the story of just one small town in Germany—Sumte. Its population at the beginning of 2015 was one hundred and two people. The town lies just east of what used to be the border between West Germany and East Germany. In early October 2015 Sumte's Mayor, Christian Fabel, received an email from the federal government informing him that one thousand Syrian refugees were being resettled into his village. He thought it was a joke. Evidently, it was not. After strenuous negotiations, the Mayor managed to cut the number down to seven hundred and fifty refugees. Let us try to capture that: seven hundred and fifty Muslim refugees coming into a village of one hundred and two people. Only nations with suicidal tendencies, led by traitors to Judeo-Christian foundations, would foist something like this on their fellow countrymen. But this is what is happening in Europe.

After the manifest disaster of Chancellor Merkel's high-handed acceptance of more than one million Muslim refugees in 2015, she had this to say on August 28, 2016. In the aftermath of a European Union Summit, and after a meeting she had with the "Visegrad Four" (Hungary, Slovakia, the Czech Republic, and Poland), which have closed their borders to Muslim refugees:

"What I still say doesn't work is for some countries to say, 'We don't want Muslims at all, even if it's necessary for humanitarian reasons."

Ever stubborn, ever ostrich-like, Mrs. Merkel, used the pulpit of her office as Chancellor to destroy the cultural and Christian character of Europe. Only one who hates who they are can be so stubborn and stupid.

Many times our political leaders scold us when we object to this flood of an alien culture that preaches our destruction to its adherents. We are told that not to accept refugees is a sin. We are told "that is not who we are." The proper response ought to be: "No, this is who we are! We are nations of Christians and Jews who do not wish to lose their bearings. THIS is who WE are!"

We may well ask ourselves how it is that more than 1.5 million can arrive as "irregular" refugees to the shores of Europe and remain there. What regime of laws, or legal limitations, makes such a situation possible?

The answer can be found in the *Handbook on European Law Relating to Asylum, Borders, and Immigration*, 2014 Edition, published by the European Union Agency For Fundamental Rights.

What is an "asylum seeker" under EU laws? It is someone who cannot return or be returned to their country of origin because they have a well-founded fear of persecution or are at risk of being ill treated or of being subjected to other serious harm. Thus, even an undocumented but well-founded "fear of persecution" is sufficient to make a refugee a legal asylum seeker.

The Asylum Procedures Directive (2013/32/EU) further provides in its Article 9(1) that the asylum seeker's presence in a EU territory is lawful. The asylum seeker is "allowed to remain in the Member State" until a decision by the competent Authority has been made on his asylum application.

Furthermore, the asylum seeker has the right to EU documentation under the Reception Conditions Directive (2013/33/EU). The Directive states that all those who seek asylum must, within three days of filing an application, be given a document certifying their status as asylum seekers. With that document in hand, most of the asylum seekers arriving in Greece would board trains to Germany, France, and Sweden, and disappear into the European heartland.

Chapter 3

ISLAM IN AMERICA TODAY

We will open this chapter with a pertinent reference to the Muslim Brotherhood's archive, accidentally discovered in the United States in 2005 by the FBI in the basement of an MB operative in Virginia. The archive was authenticated and introduced by the Federal Government as evidence at the trial of the Holy Land Foundation case in Dallas in November 2008. Titled "An Explanatory Memorandum For the General Strategic Goal in North America" and written in May 1991, it reads as follows (Page 4, paragraph 4):

> "The process of settlement is a 'Civilization Jihadist Process' with all the word means. The Ikhwan (i.e. the Muslim faithful) must understand that their work in America is a kind of grand jihad in eliminating and destroying the Western civilization from within and 'sabotaging' its miserable house by the hands of the believers so that it is eliminated and God's religion is made victorious over all religions."

What could better meet these criteria than America and Europe's own laws, which have enabled the wholesale invasion of the European and the North American continent by its historical enemies?

Federal District Judge Solis, who presided over the Holy Land Foundation case, ordered at the end of the trial that a List of Unindicted Co-conspirators be published. These co-conspirators are all persons or organizations that had assisted Holy Land Foundation in perpetrating its fundraising-for-terrorism scheme in the U.S. The most prominent Muslim-American civic organizations, which have regular access to the White House, are all on that list. For example, the Council on American Islamic Relations (CAIR) is listed in Part III of the list, under the heading: "The following are individuals/entities who are or were members of the U.S Palestine Committee and/or its organizations." The Islamic Society of North America (ISNA) is listed in Part VII of the co-conspirators list under the heading: "The following are individuals/entities who are and/or were members of the U.S. Muslim Brotherhood."

The Explanatory Memorandum makes it clear in a five-point strategic plan that Islam is to be "settled," i.e. established in the United States and that at the appropriate time, and if necessary, violence and force are to be used to establish Sharia law as the only law of the land. Hassan al-Banna, the founder of the Muslim Brotherhood in 1928, had called for mosques to be used the same way the Prophet had used them: as power centers for his movement and as armories for their arms, which were then repeatedly used to conquer other Arab tribes from within. True to form, therefore, the Explanatory Memorandum calls in paragraph 11 for each mosque to have its "Security Organization," which is to include:

a) "Clubs for training and learning self-defense techniques"

b) "A center which is concerned with security issues (technical, intellectual, technological, and human)... and things like that."

According to the FBI, there are twenty-two Islamic paramilitary training camps in the United States. Most are affiliated with an organization called Muslims of America (MOA), which is in turn affiliated with Jamaat ul-Fuqra, a Pakistani Muslim Brotherhood affiliate. In Florida, for example, there are three such camps—in Ft. Lauderdale, Orlando, and Tampa. Is this any surprise? Even Muslim women are said to be receiving paramilitary training at these camps. Do we all remember Mr. Farooq's wife's proficiency with assault weapons in the San Bernardino massacre?

Josh Siegel, News Editor of *The Daily Signal*, in an article dated April 16, 2016 on Houston's Muslim community, gives us the following additional national statistics to help us better understand the Muslim presence in America. Muslims represent:

> Ten percent of all legally arriving immigrants
>
> Sixty-five percent of them are Sunni, and eleven percent identify as Shia

Fifty-one percent are millennials (young people), thirty-one percent Generation X'ers, and fifteen percent Baby Boomers.

Of all Muslims in America:

Sixty-four percent are immigrants (enormous percentage). Seventeen percent second generation. Eighteen percent third generation.

Forty-eight percent have done college work, or hold a college degree, while thirty-six percent only have a high school education.

Thirty-four percent have household incomes of under $30,000, and eighty percent do not exceed household income of $50,000.

This means that most of America's Muslims are foreign-born immigrants, coming from harsh and unforgiving cultures, and they are young people, with lower income brackets. Unfortunately, Mr. Siegel does not give us statistics on the male/female makeup, though the experience of the San Bernardino massacre shows us that women can also be vicious terrorists in the cause of Allah.

In my earlier book originally published in 2010 titled *Islam vs. The United States*, we reviewed the history of Islam's relations with and presence in the United States. We exposed how the young American Republic's first war on foreign soil was against the Muslim pirates from the Barbary Coast. We also looked into biblical references to the sons of Hagar and Ishmael, now known as the Arab tribes, which are predominantly Muslim. Given the above, the scope of this chapter is to update our readers on the present state of affairs in the United States.

By most counts, though lots of contradictory figures are put out, the total number of Muslims in the U.S. presently stands at about 3.3 million. There are also approximately two thousand two hundred mosques and/or Islamic centers operating in the U.S.

Islamic expansion has been taking place here under two main thrusts: violent jihad and civilization jihad. Violent jihad is harder to measure in its success, because its main element is fear—our fear of becoming a target, our fear even of political retribution from the misguided forces of the left. The left has willfully chosen to blind itself to what Sharia really is: the demotion of women to the status of property, the absolute intolerance of homosexuality, a brutal code of punishment for the most innocuous crimes, and a tolerance of laws that contradict our Constitution. Civilization jihad has been progressing in the United

States, thanks to the efforts of the more than one thousand different organizations that the Muslim Brotherhood has set up in this country, led by the Council on American Islamic Relations (CAIR), the Islamic Society of North America (ISNA), the Muslim Student's Association (MSA), which has branches on more than seven hundred college campuses, and others.

America is referred to by both the Shia and Sunni branches of Islam as "the Great Satan." The use of this moniker achieves the dual purpose of setting up Islam as a force that is morally superior to the U.S., and fires up the imagination of impressionable young men who begin as repenters from sin and sincere God-seekers and end up as vicious killers of those who are not Muslim.

Why do the forces of Islam refer to America as "the Great Satan"? The reasons are several. Without meaning to set an order of importance, let us say that America's support of Israel, America's liberal laws and culture in condoning violent music, pornography, homosexuality, equality of the sexes, rap, pop artists etc., all hit a raw nerve in the Muslim psyche. The self-assumed status of a morally superior Islam, however, does not match the reality on the ground. Muslim countries from Saudi Arabia, to Iran, to Pakistan, to Afghanistan and others share the same problems we have. The only difference is that their problems are buried below a shallow surface and supposedly do not exist.

I have a message for all imams: Satan does not exclusively assault America. He assaults all nations, all people, all families, and all faiths. As God-seekers, which is also what I am, imams must know like I know that Satan is ruthless. He attacks the whole human race. America has lots of men of God who stand against Satan. I am one of them. America is not the Great Satan any more than anyone else. There is a battle in America against the forces of Satan, just as there is in Muslim countries.

And imams and Islamic clergy DO NOT have a monopoly on being men of God. Christian clergy and Jewish clergy fight the same battles to keep their spiritual flock away from Satan's attacks.

The Muslim world has its homosexuals, its pornography addicts, and its drug-infested pop musicians. It also has its women who rightfully dream of equality with men. Muslims simply suppress with violent means these parts of their society. But in addition to that, and unlike Western societies, they have honor killings, enslaved women, genetic defects due to constant intermarriage between first cousins in the Arab world, and limitations on human imagination and thinking that have led to almost complete stagnation in the sciences and technological development. In addition to all this, they are called to observe and defend a religion, which does not include one single eyewitness testimony or proof of a miracle. Christianity offers its supporters almost constant proof of miracles, from the Holy Light phenomenon which occurs before one hundred thousand faithful on Good Saturday every Orthodox Easter at the Church of the Holy Sepulcher in Jerusalem, to constant miracles that we all know of or hear of performed by our Lord in clinics, churches, and our everyday life. All this is in addition to the eyewitness documented miracles we read of in the Old and New Testaments, the miracle of Enoch being taken up to heaven in the Old Testament, the ten miracles that set the Israelites free from Egypt, the miracle performed by Jesus in raising Lazarus from the dead, to the miracles performed by the apostles.

Miracles in Christianity: The Holy Light comes to the Church of the Holy Sepulcher, Jerusalem, April 2005.

So, the self-assumed role of Islam as the morally superior religion is not matched with the facts on the ground. I am reminded of the testimony of a Shia friend, Farzad, whose grandfather was an Ayatollah in

Iran. My friend was placed in an exclusive madrassah at a young age, led by an eighty-five-plus year old imam. The students did everything they could think of to please Allah. They denied themselves even the simple rudiments of living, like food and sleep. They slept on hard floors, and sometimes even on broken glass, all to please Allah with their commitment. After two years Farzad asked to see the imam. He was coldly received and asked why he wanted to see him. My friend said words to the effect that he had been at the madrassah already for two years, had carried out all sorts of self-sacrifice, and yet had heard nothing from Allah. The imam angrily ordered him to get out, and as he was doing so yelled at him that he had been doing the same thing for seventy-two years and had not heard from Allah. Contrast that to the grace and mercy that our Lord Jesus casts on us daily, from the moment we come to Him. Contrast it also to the proven knowledge of miracles that our Lord gives us constantly.

It is not easy to be a Muslim. My heart goes out to so many young people in Islamic countries who are seeking God, sacrifice to show Him they want to be His, and hear nothing back from Him. What they do hear is from their imams, and it is almost always violent. What is it, after all, that makes a young man in the prime of his age strap dynamite to his body and blow himself and innocent others up? This is the tragedy of the young God-seekers who are raised with violent teachings.

Now let us redirect our attention at the work carried out in the United States by the forces of civilization jihad. ISNA tells its members that every Muslim household must have a copy of *The Umdat al Salik*, the book known in the West as *Reliance of the Traveller*. This is the handbook for every practicing Muslim. Written by Ahmad ibn Naqib al-Misri, who died in 1368 AD, this book interprets and codifies the Koran into a whole life-system. But here is the problem for

Islam: when you preach a whole-life system that covers the spiritual, the religious, the political, the financial, the legal, and the hygienic aspects of life, you must not be angry when you receive criticism from non-believers in Islam on ANY of those fronts. Islam has set itself up for this all-encompassing life system. Perhaps it tries to do too much. By contrast, Christianity teaches something different: it does not mix the spiritual with the secular. Jesus said: "Give unto Caesar what is Caesar's, and give unto God what is God's."

Now back to *Reliance of the Traveller*: It is the highest authority on Islamic jurisprudence in the world and is certified by Al-Azhar University in Egypt, the foremost academic institution on Islam. The book begins by affirming in a1.4 that:

> "the good is not what reason considers good,
> nor is the bad what reason considers bad."
> And
> "...the good of the acts of those who are morally
> responsible is what the Lawgiver (i.e. Allah) or His
> messenger (Mohammed) has indicated is good by
> permitting it or asking that it be done."

Under this teaching, therefore, if Mohammed "consummated" his marriage with Aisha when she was only nine years old, this is good. And if mere mortals passed laws (like the U.S. Constitution) that did not come from Allah or his messenger, this is bad. The book goes on to instruct in b7.3: "Oh you who believe, obey Allah and obey the Prophet, and those of authority among you." (Koran 4:59)

Therefore, when an imam tells a young man he will go to Jinnah (Paradise) if he blows himself up, the young man must obey.

There are other troubling aspects of Islam that are totally incongruous with our Judeo-Christian values and our laws. For example, the treatment of women and even underage girls as sex objects and sex slaves. This all has its roots in Islam's tradition of plunder and rape, and in the Sunnah, the examples to be followed that Mohammed himself set with what he did in his life. Sura 65.4 permits marriage with pre-pubescent girls, Sura 4:3 allows marriage with multiple women, and Sura 4:34 permits the beating of wives.

Reliance of the Traveller also teaches, as part of Sharia law, that "retaliation is obligatory against anyone who kills a human being purely intentionally and without right. And it adds that "those not subject to retaliation" (i.e. not be punished for a killing) include "a father or mother (or their fathers and mothers) for killing their offspring, or offspring's offspring" (see Umdat al-Salik, *Book Of Justice*, 01.1-2).

By the way, let us note that there are many cases of "justified" (or approved) killings in Islam, including for blasphemy against Islam, leaving Islam for another religion, etc.

I can hardly imagine the Archangel Gabriel imparting these teachings to Mohammed. Can you?

All the above are acts which are specifically illegal in the United States, and in almost all Western European countries.

Reliance of the Traveller also enjoins in paragraph a4.2 the Umma (the faithful) "to refrain from discussing subtleties of scholastic theology, lest corruption difficult to eliminate find its way into their basic religious conviction."

It calls for "jihad," which it defines as: "to war on against non-Muslims… signifying warfare to establish Islam" and that it is "obligatory for every Muslim."

This is the book, together with the Koran, that the Islamic Society of North America (ISNA) wants in every Muslim-American home. And this is what Muslim children are taught in the U.S. in an obligatory book they are given at their mosques titled, *What Islam Is All About*.

There is no version of Islam that contradicts these teachings. Where is teaching in Islam of peace and love to all people? In Christianity love is the basic command. The labeling of Islam by its followers as "the religion of peace" is just not true. The opposite is true. Islam divides the world into two camps: the Dar al Islam (the house of Islam where Sharia governs), and the Dar al Harb (the House of War, where Islam does not yet prevail). Peace actually does not prevail in the Dar al Islam nor in the Dar al Harb. In the former bloody fights between Sunni and Shia, and in the latter other religions, the forces of Islam are fighting bloody battles. The United States belongs in the Dar al Harb.

Repeated and vicious terrorist attacks continue to take place in the U.S. I will not go into the litany of the dead, dismembered, and psychologically traumatized victims Islam has left in its path in America. Law enforcement, beginning in the Bush Administration and continuing with the Obama Administration, have erroneously placed their hopes in obtaining the cooperation of the Muslim community itself in alerting the authorities to possible acts of Islamic terror. This really is almost a vain hope. John Guandolo, a former special agent of the FBI in counter-terrorism and founder of Understanding the Threat, sets forth Koranic verses and teachings from the Hadith (the sayings of Mohammed) which clearly condemn "talebearing," a crime under Islam. For example, Sura 49:12 instructs: "Do not slander (spy on) one another." Mohammed is said to have instructed, "the talebearer will not enter paradise. " Sharia law defines "talebearing" as follows: "The reality of talebearing lies in divulging a secret, in revealing something confidential, whose disclosure is resented."

The combination of Islamic prohibition on talebearing, and the fear that our political leaders have imposed on our people through political correctness and fear of being labeled a "racist" have led to the death of Americans. For example, neighbors of the San Bernardino terrorists had seen evidence of bomb making in their apartment, but were afraid to call the police for fear of being called racist.

At the same time, political leaders like Madame Clinton have assured the public repeatedly that "Islam has nothing to do with terrorism." But Islam has everything to do with terrorism. President Obama has done his share in this misinformation campaign by claiming that the terrorists are not Muslims, a claim absurd on its face when they constantly invoke Islam and the Koran as they murder and maim people.

Some of our senior political leaders are compromised by the forces of Islam. Richard Pollock of the *Daily Caller* reports that former President Bill Clinton served from 2011 to 2014 as Honorary Chairman of GEMS Education, a Dubai-based Islamic school chain that operates more than one hundred schools in the Middle East, Asia, and Africa. He also collected, according to the Clinton's tax returns, more than $5.6 million in fees from GEMS.

The FBI's Deputy Assistant Director for the Weapons of Mass Destruction Program from 2006 to 2012 was an Iranian-born Muslim, Dr. Vahid Majidi. He now serves in the Obama Administration as Deputy Assistant Secretary of Defense for Nuclear Matters. What vetting process has a man with obvious background risks like him gone through?

Recently, Senators John McCain (R-AZ), Lindsey Graham (R-SC), and Richard Blumenthal (D-CT) gave an award to a certain Mr.

Abdelhakim Belhadj for good citizenship. They wanted to recognize him as a "moderate Muslim." But Mr. Belhadj is a well-known jihadist, who was even the subject of a CIA "rendition" and spent seven years in a Libyan jail for his jihadist activities. Now he is in America receiving good citizenship awards. Another Al Amoudi in the making?

When will this sheer idiocy, if not treachery, end?

Some of our most prestigious universities, including Harvard, Princeton, Georgetown, and George Mason University have Islamic Studies departments, which are financed and were founded with mega donations from the representatives of civilization jihad. Professors in these programs blithely continue the misinformation campaign, turning our universities that used to be beacons of biblical truth into mouthpieces for Islam.

Two members of the U.S. House of Representatives, Keith Ellison (D, MN) and Andre Carson (D, IN) are Muslim. Though Members of Congress are sworn by the Speaker en masse by just raising their right hand, representative Ellison made it a point after he took his oath of office in January 2007 to pose with Speaker Nancy Pelosi holding the copy of Jefferson's Koran. Jefferson, to be sure, studied the Koran not because he agreed with it but because he was a learned man. For Pelosi and Ellison to try to confuse the issue and make it look like Jefferson somehow approved of the Koran is typical of the twisting and misrepresentation that our political leaders carry on almost daily. Even President Bush, in the aftermath of 9/11, said that Islam is the religion of peace.

So, let us be clear: all Federal officers, including Senators, Members of the House, the President, and Vice President must take an Oath or make an Affirmation that they "will support this Constitution" (U.S. Constitution, Article VI). Article VI also states that the Constitution "is the supreme law of the land." This same article also states that all judges are bound by its provisions. How can a practicing Muslim, who believes in the Koran and its spiritual child Sharia law, ever affirm that he places the United States Constitution above Islamic laws? The very idea of a fully practicing Muslim's affirmation that he will uphold the Constitution is an oxymoron. This is the truth.

At the Democratic National Convention in July 2016, prominence was given to Mr. Khizr Khan, an immigrant from Pakistan whose son was a captain in the U.S. Army and was killed in action. Mr. Khan, with great fanfare and hypocrisy, waived a copy of the U.S. Constitution over his head and accused Mr. Trump of not knowing what it says. He also accused Mr. Trump of having "sacrificed nothing." Great theater! If sacrificing something was the applicable criterion, did Mr. Khan ask Hillary Clinton what she and her husband have sacrificed? And was he waving the Constitution by way of telling us that he places it above the Koran? I do not think he does! So then why does invoking a document that he personally does not believe to be the supreme law of the land? Lastly, what evidence did Mr. Khan have to support his accusation that Donald Trump does not know what it says?

Subsequent investigation by some in the media has shown that Mr. Khan's single partner law firm specializes in bringing in Muslim immigrants into the U.S. When this was discovered, he pulled his law firm's homepage off the internet in a vain attempt to conceal what he does for a living. It also transpired that prior to setting up his single partner law firm, he worked at a big law firm with very strong Democrat ties that does extensive work for the Clintons. The Khan incident is typical of the misinformation campaign being conducted by the representatives of civilization jihad to bamboozle the American public. We now hear, for example, that Trump disrespects gold star families. Nothing could be farther from the truth. He respects the sacrifice of gold star families, and the Khans are not a typical gold star family. They have a secret agenda. It is to promote another religion and culture, which are in opposition to our Judeo-Christian civilization.

The sad thing about those who organize or support such misinformation campaigns is that this is not politics; it is "aiding and abetting the enemy."

On December 10, 2015 the new judge of the 7th Municipal District of New York, Carolyn Walker-Diallo, took her Oath of Office on the Koran. One of her duties as a judge is to uphold the U.S. Constitution and the duties it imposes upon the States, including the State of New York. How can she logically be trusted to do this when her Oath of Office was taken on an alien body of laws?

It is clear that such practices must be discontinued. It is politically correct nonsense! As we mentioned above, the Constitution permits an Oath or an Affirmation. If the public official being sworn in does not wish to do so on the Bible or the Torah, then they must take their Oath on the U.S. Constitution. But they must no longer be permitted to take their Oath on the Koran, which is so antithetical to the Constitution. And those who have assumed public office already by using the Koran must be obliged by law to retake their Oath of Office on the U.S. Constitution. It is neither "cool" nor amusing to have people play hard and fast with the bedrock foundations of our Republic and in the process confuse and corrupt principles. These principles took so much blood and sacrifice to achieve and led to the establishment of the greatest republic in the world's history. "Cool" does not cut it when compared to the wonder that is our Constitution and our Republic!

I wish to emphasize that a Christian and a Jew do not face the same dilemma, namely, which governs their book of faith or the U.S.

Constitution. Why? Because the entire U.S. Constitution is based on biblical principles contained in the Old and in the New Testaments, from the Ten Commandments to the concept that man's rights are God-given and not government or man-given. So it is practicing Muslims only who face the dilemma: the Koran or the U.S. Constitution? How can this dilemma ever be resolved?

Captain Joseph John (USN, ret) is an expert who tracks all inroads made in the U.S. by the various front organizations of the Muslim Brotherhood. Joined by John Guandolo of Understanding The Threat, Lt. General Jerry Boykin (USA, ret), Frank Gaffney of the Center For Security Policy and other experts, they provide an invaluable patriotic service to our country. Pressure has been mounting to end the liberal licentiousness that is leading to the dissolution of the Judeo-Christian foundations of the United States. These patriots are aware of and see through the instruction of the Koran (Sura 3:28) that when you are not powerful enough, you may temporarily strike alliances with the infidels until you are strong enough to take over. This has been the tried and tested model of Muslim inroads into the laws and culture of Europe. To help stem such a tide in the United States, certain politicians have proposed appropriate legislation.

One such House Bill, HR 3892, proposed by Representative Mario Diaz-Balart (R-FL) designates the Muslim Brotherhood as a terrorist organization and calls for deporting from the U.S. all foreign nationals who are members of the MB. It does not, however, reach U.S citizens who may be members of the MB or one of its front organizations. Such a law needs now to be enacted. America must remain a beacon of freedom, hope, and security to the rest of the world.

President Obama has certainly and gleefully contributed to the rise of Islam in America. His intentions ought not to have been misinterpreted or misunderstood. In his book *Audacity of Hope*, written prior to his election as President, he states: "I will stand with Muslims should the political winds shift in an ugly direction."

Obama's favor for Muslim causes, which has been reported widely (though not by the mainstream media), is exemplified by two cases. The first is the adoption by the Equal Employment Opportunity Commission of new rules for private employers that invoke and re-interpret Title VII of the Civil Rights Act on workplace discrimination. The EEOC order states that American employers must accommodate the religious needs of Muslims and ensure that they are not being harassed or intimidated. As is typical of his Administration, Obama's EEOC promulgated these new rules immediately after the San Bernardino massacre. Never leave a tragedy unexploited! So now, if a Muslim truck driver objects to delivering alcoholic beverages to his company's clients, he must be excused. Prayer breaks during work hours must be accommodated on company time. Several companies in Nebraska, California, and Colorado were thus coerced by the EEOC. Naturally, the cost of any litigation the EEOC brings to enforce this new interpretation of the Civil Rights Act is borne by the taxpayers. So now we, the taxpayers, are paying to help impose a Muslim agenda on America. Orwellian, isn't it?

In the immediate aftermath of the San Bernardino massacre, the chairwoman of the EEOC, Jenny R. Yang, in fact stated that Muslims are "vulnerable communities" requiring Federal protection "even as we grapple with the concerns raised by the recent terrorist attacks." Her agency ends its notice by inviting Muslims to file anti-discrimination complaints if they feel mistreated. Not a word about how the EEOC would concentrate in the future on protecting workplaces in America like the Dan Bernardino county engineer's office from the likes of Mr.

Farook, the San Bernardino assassin! The cynicism and callousness of the Obama Administration are offensive and must be redressed with determination and power. It is wantonly callous, and offensive laws like these lead to dictatorships. I hope and pray that does not happen in America, but ruthless extinction of such government acts is absolutely necessary.

The second example we can discuss is the Obama Administration's re-introduction of the teaching of religion in our public schools. We recall here that the 1947 Everson v. N.J. Board of Education case first established (by completely and willfully misinterpreting the First Amendment) that there must be "an impregnable wall of separation between Church and State." That decision was followed in 1962 by the Engel v. Vitale decision of the U.S. Supreme Court that outlawed the teaching of religion, the showing of the Ten Commandments, and all prayer (even private prayer on public school property). But along comes the Obama Administration and encourages the teaching of religion, for extra credit, in America's public schools. Which religion, you might wonder? Not Christianity and not Judaism, but Islam. Schools in Arizona, Maryland, and Michigan have already begun this extra credit program in Islamic religious studies. But why, then, are Christianity and Judaism not taught in our public schools for extra credit?

Chapter 4

THE "ESTABLISHMENT OF RELIGION" CLAUSE OF THE FIRST AMMENDMENT

One has to wonder when looking at the entire picture of what the Obama Administration has done, whether it is running afoul of the restrictions of the "establishment" clause of the First Amendment about the separation of Church and State. This landmark decision was handed down by in the Everson v. New Jersey Board of Education case by the Supreme Court in 1947.

In it, Justice Hugo Black, writing for the majority, said the following: "The establishment clause of the First Amendment means at least this: that no State nor the Federal Government can set up a church, neither can pass laws, which aid one religion, aid all religions, nor prefer one religion over another."

I disagree with this decision, as I have explained in detail in my book *Bring Down That Wall*. Plainly speaking, Justice Black and his cohorts in this decision invented and added language that is just not in the First Amendment. The "establishment clause" simply says,

"Congress shall make no law with regard to the establishment of a religion, or the free exercise thereof...." It says nothing about State of Local Government in the United States, or of any constraint on them regarding religion. The Founders were clear that they only meant to prevent the Federal Government from establishing a national religion. Religion, in their view, was a State's right, and would be decided by each State.

However, having made this decision and established into the law of the land the principle that no government (Federal, State, or Local) could "aid one religion" or "prefer one religion over another," how can the EEOC decision on the Muslim truck drivers or the re-introduction of only Islamic religious teaching in America's public schools be reconciled with the reasoning and constrictions of the Everson ruling?

Why is it legal for a Muslim to impose his religion upon the company that employs him and the fellow workers whom he inconveniences with his prayer breaks and refusal to deliver alcoholic beverages? Is that not approving and aiding one religion, while suppressing others? Is not the teaching only of Islam, for extra credit, at our public schools not aiding and preferring one religion over another?

And why is it illegal for a baker who objects to homosexual marriage to refuse to bake a cake for such a wedding ceremony? Why is the Muslim entitled to impose his religious views on his company and co-workers, but a Christian baker cannot even refuse to bake a cake that his prospective client can order in any number of other stores?

The "establishment of religion" interdiction on Congress contained in the First Amendment obliges Congress to prevent any effort to establish a religion. When Muslims in America demand, and mostly receive permission for, such rights as we have described above, are they not attempting to "establish a religion"? Where is Congress to intervene, as is its duty, to prohibit such efforts to establish a religion, namely the religion of Islam? And where is our Executive, which has a duty to enforce our laws, and the judiciary, which has a duty to interpret our laws according to our Constitution, to intervene with such practices and enforce the provisions of the First Amendment? Or is it that the interdiction of the "establishment of religion" clause is only to be applied against Christians and Jews?

On September 25, 2009 a Muslim prayer ceremony was held on Federal property on the west side of the U.S. Capitol with fifty thousand Muslims in attendance. Isn't Government permission required to hold an event at this site? The same site where U.S Presidents have been taking the Oath of Office since 1981? And this permission was given by the Federal Government even though in May 2009 President Obama canceled the 21st National Prayer Day because he did not want "to offend anyone." Isn't this aiding one religion over another?

What has happened here is so typical of liberal-progressive tactics and the judicial activists who support them. They will twist and turn everyone and everything that used to be a clear principle, until everyone looks at an "eight" and thinks like a "zero." That is what is happening in the U.S.

This is why I say that such rules must be expunged with power and ruthlessness if we are to save this Republic and keep it true to its origins and its original intent.

One more point for those of my readers who may think of our Constitution as an antiquated document. First, it is the law of the land, indeed the Supreme Law of the land. Second, it contains provisions for amending it. They require 2/3 of both Houses of Congress and ¾ of all the State Legislatures. It has, in fact, been amended twenty-seven times, which is why we have twenty-seven Amendments. But is cannot ever be amended by cavalier impostors who take it upon themselves to sidestep its provisions and do as they like, either with illegal Executive Orders (as Obama has done) or by refusing to bring Bills to the Senate floor and paralyzing the political process (as former Senate Majority Leader Harry Reid did).

Chapter 5

THE MUSLIM REFUGEE RESETTLEMENT PROGRAM

Since completely failing to contain the civil war in Syria, the Obama Administration has once again cynically concentrated on turning yet another crisis that is its responsibility into an opportunity to promote Islam in America.

First, I wish to be clear about a principal point: I am in favor of re-settling refugees in the U.S., even some Muslim refugees, *if* they can give initial and continuing evidence that they truly respect this country, its institutions, laws, and Judeo-Christian foundations. That would require stringent tests. The United States is under no obligation to import refugees, especially when their backgrounds cannot be checked and when their co-religionists in the Arabian Gulf area (Saudi Arabia, Qatar, the United Arab Emirates, and others) refuse to take them. If their co-religionists do not welcome them, why must the United States? I have come to suspect and disagree with the unwarranted sense of pride that Western politicians' exhibit, anxious as they are to appear ever so humanitarian and upstanding when lecturing the rest of us on our "duties" to receive refugees. Instead of focusing so much energy on imposing on their own doubting domestic populations the need to accept refugees, why do our politicians not focus their energy on letting these people into fellow Muslim countries. The true refugees from Syria should principally be the Christians who are trying to keep safe from the Syrian Resistance (who are heavily ISIS-controlled). How many Christian refugees have been accepted into Europe and the U.S., compared to Muslim refugees?

But since the Syrian refugee crisis began, how could the liberal-progressive forces allow such a golden opportunity to make money and gain more power pass?

Let us look at the case of the International Rescue Committee (IRC), an NGO that has ties to George Soros and the Clintons. The IRC was set up to operate as a government contractor to help resettle refuges. Its president and CEO, up until 2015, was David Miliband, the former Foreign Secretary of the United Kingdom from 2007 to 2010, and a great friend of the Clintons. Bill Clinton has been quoted saying that Miliband is "one of the ablest, most creative public servants of our time." After he quit politics in 2013 in his native Britain, Miliband assumed the CEO's job at the IRC.

IRC, according to its website, participates as a Federal Government contractor in refugee resettlement programs, including resettlement into twenty-six cities in the U.S. Seeking to pressure the U.S. into accepting a fresh group of one hundred thousand refugees, Miliband authored an article in the *New York Daily News* on June 20, 2016 titled, "Refugees Are An Asset, Not A Threat." For his services to IRC he has been drawing a salary of more than $350,000 per year.

Sounds great, does it not?

Well, the U.S. Agency for International Development has placed the IRC and Mr. Miliband under investigation and suspended tens of millions of dollars worth of aid for Syrian refugees. The Inspector General of the USAID commenced in May 2016 an official investigation. The Inspector General said, "it had established grounds" for the suspension of tens of millions of dollars in aid flowing through these entities. According to the announcement made at the time, IRC was involved in bid rigging and working with service and equipment providers in Turkey who were inflating their bills. The spokesman for the IG's office said, "What became clear in the course of this investigation was this is a pretty sophisticated operation."

According to an article written on May 16, 2016 by Captain Joseph John (USN, ret), the Obama Administration has already resettled nine hundred fifteen thousand Muslim refugees in one hundred eighty U.S. cities. Obama's Immigration Advisor at the White House, Cecilia Munoz, has openly referred to these refugees as "seedlings" that they are planting in various communities. Seedlings are meant to grow. And they are growing at taxpayer expense, against the background of the FBI's self-admitted inability to properly vet them. This is suicidal. The question is, what is behind it? Why is this happening? The IRC, until the time of its suspension, had planted seedling communities in twenty-six areas within the U.S., including Atlanta, Wichita, Baltimore, Boise, Dallas, Miami, Salt Lake City, San Diego, Seattle, Tucson, Phoenix, Los Angeles, Charlottesville (VA), Silver Springs (MD), and northern California. All this while the liberal establishment placed highly paid "friends" into key positions in the refugee resettlement NGO's. The IRC alone had collected more than $380 million in grants from the Federal Government before its suspension. According to Captain John, in some communities like Troy and Sterling Heights,

MI these NGO's were resettling the very few Christians who have been admitted as refugees right next to Islamic "refugees" whose tender mercies those poor Christians had been trying to escape when they left the war zones.

Together with their problems, the Muslim refugees bring with them their long tradition of honor killings. Understanding the Threat, led by former FBI Special Agent John Guandolo, tracks honor killings in the U.S.—killings that somehow we never hear about from the liberal media. In a recent article, UTT gives us the following examples of honor killings:

- In April 2004, a Turkish Muslim killed his 4-year old daughter in Scottsdale, NY because she had been "sullied" by a gynecological exam.
- In 2006, a Somali immigrant in Kentucky brutally killed his four children and raped his wife because he suspected her of infidelity.
- In January 2008, an Egyptian Muslim shot and killed his two daughters in Irving, TX. The girls' aunt told reporters these were "honor killings."
- In July 2008, a Pakistani Muslim in Atlanta, GA killed his daughter because she refused an arranged marriage.
- In October 2009, an Iraqi Muslim in Arizona drove his car over his daughter for being "too Westernized." She died two weeks later.
- In October 2009, a Muslim woman in New Brighton, NY attempted to kill her husband by slitting his throat because he was not "Muslim enough."

The Department of Justice reports there are approximately twenty-seven honor killings each year in the U.S.

Why does America need to be exposed to this? Never before in its history did America allow itself to be put in such a position. Immigrants, including Swedes, Irishmen, Greeks, Italians, Koreans, Chinese, and many others all came here with respect in their souls for America, for its way of life, and for its laws. Never before has the public allowed its politicians to scold us over obvious dangers like this and tell us that this "is not who we are." This is a disgrace. So who exactly are we? Are we some kind of new breed that must accustom itself to Islamic terror, to honor killings, and to the corruption of our laws and our Constitution? Is that who our politicians want us to be? And if so, why?

I close this chapter by reminding us all that according to Mr. Trump, Madame Clinton wants to increase by five hundred fifty percent the number of refugees coming into the United States. I ask again, why?

Chapter 6

SURVEYS ON MUSLIM ATTITUDES (Not a pretty picture)

Islam is unlike any other religion in the world. As has been said by any authoritative sources, it is a world-domination and whole-life system that includes politics, culture, justice, and war codes. Under Sharia there is no separation of religion, politics, and the duty to wage war. As such, it must be recognized by nations who harbor Muslim populations that Islam cannot and must not be seen only as a religion. Once that is understood, then it will be easier to recognize that Islam cannot be accorded the typical "freedom of religion" rights that other religions receive. Religion is expected to cover only the spiritual. When, however, it encroaches on all the other matters included under Islam, and when it threatens the common laws of its host countries, not to mention the physical security of the host country's citizens, then we have to say that limits need to be placed on Islam's teaching and methods. The Western view that mosques are just a Muslim church is so wrong that it is silly.

In Egypt, just after the Muslim Brotherhood had taken over the country and installed Mohammed Morsi as its new President, one of the leading clerics, Yusuf al Qaradawi, issued a Fatwa (Islamic legal ruling) that answered the question: "Is it permissible to use a mosque for political purposes?" His Fatwa states:

"It must be the role of the mosque to guide the public policy of a nation, raise awareness of critical issues, and reveal its enemies. From ancient times the mosque has had a role in urging jihad for the sake of Allah, resisting the enemies of the religion who are invading occupiers.

That blessed intifada in the land of the prophet, Palestine, started from none other than the mosques."

The Islamic President of Turkey, Recep Erdogan, said in a famous speech in 2002: "The mosques are our barracks, the domes our helmets, the minarets our bayonets, and the faithful our soldiers."

So, let us ask ourselves, what is the role of more than two thousand two hundred mosques and Islamic centers operating in the United States? Do they have the same role as a Christian church or a synagogue? Or does their role expand into sedition and anti-constitutional activity? Are Donald Trump, Senator Ted Cruz, and Dr. Ben Carson prejudiced bigots and racists when they call, as they did in the 2016 Primary Campaign, for close monitoring of mosques in America?

Islam teaches the principle of "loyalty and enmity." What this generally means is that Muslims who are in the minority in a country must show loyalty where they cannot do otherwise, but retain their enmity toward their rulers so that they can one day take them over. Koranic Suras that teach the principle of perpetual enmity toward the infidel include 4:89, 4:144, 5:51, 5:54, 6:40, 9:23, and 60:1. For an example of this principle, we may all recall stories of surprised Christians, Jews, and Yazidis living in lands that were subsequently taken over by ISIS when they found out that their Muslims neighbors, who they thought were their close friends, had betrayed them and turned them in to the new governing authorities.

Sura 4:89 reads as follows: "They (the infidels) wish you would disbelieve as they disbelieved, so you would be alike. So do not take from among them allies until they emigrate (come to) for the cause of Allah. But if they turn away (from Allah), then seize them and kill them wherever you find them and take not from among them any ally or help." (Parentheses are mine).

The Pew Research Center offers us a wealth of insights into Muslim attitudes and beliefs. Analyzing their statistics can be an eye-opening experience.

In an April 26, 2016 study and article titled, "How Much Should the Koran Influence Our Country's Laws?", the Pew Center reported that the following views were recorded:

COUNTRY	STRICTLY FOLLOW	FOLLOW VALUES	NOT BE INFLUENCED
Pakistan	78%	18%	2%
Palestine	65	23	8
Jordan	64	38	7
Malaysia	52	17	17
Senegal	49	33	16
Nigeria	27	17	42
Indonesia	22	52	16
Lebanon	15	37	42
Turkey	13	38	36

Source: Pew Research Center, Spring 2015, Global Attitudes Survey, Q24

The Pew Center estimates from a 2011 survey that there were 2,750,000 Muslims in the U.S., of whom 1,800,000 were adults, and sixty-three percent were immigrants to the U.S. Between 2010 and 2050, Pew estimates that the Muslim population worldwide will increase by seventy-three percent, while Christian populations will increase by only thirty-five percent, Hindus by thirty-four percent, and Jews by sixteen percent. Thus, the immigrants predominate in the Muslim population of the U.S. bring with them attitudes from their countries of origin, which are dangerous, as the table above shows.

Another Pew Research Center study, reported in 2013 (http://www.pewforum.org/2013/04/30/the-worlds-muslims-religion-politics-society-overview/) asked whether Muslims wanted Sharia law to be the official law of the land. Here are some of the country-by-country results:

COUNTRY	PERCENTAGE OF MUSLIMS WHO WANT SHARIA
Afghanistan	99
Iraq	91
Palestine	89
Pakistan	84
Egypt	74
Indonesia	72
Nigeria	71
Russia	42
Kosovo	20
Turkey	12
Albania	12
Kazakhstan	10
Azerbaijan	8

An extension of the same study by Pew in 2013 asked if suicide bombings and other forms of violence against civilians are rarely or never justified. Ninety-two percent of Indonesia's Muslims answered negatively (a good sign) and ninety-one percent in Iraq. In a 2011 Pew study of U.S. Muslims (http://www.pewforum.org/2013/-4/3-/the-worlds-muslims-religion-politics-society-app-a/?beta-true&utm_expid-53098246-2.Lly4CFSVQG2lphsg), eighty-six percent of American Muslims answered in the negative, but seven percent said that suicide bombings are sometimes justified, and one percent said that they are often justified. We saw earlier that America's adult Muslim population was estimated by Pew in 2011 at 1.8 million. So: seven percent of 1.8 million amounts to one hundred twenty-six thousand American Muslims who think suicide bombings are sometimes justified, and another eighteen thousand think they are "often justified."

Isn't that alarming? Which mosques are putting, or allowing, such ideas to creep in to the thinking of fellow Americans? And lastly: what can be done about this?

Certainly Mrs. Clinton's and Mr. Kane's grab-the votes-with-whatever-lie-is-necessary approach does not work and is dishonest. It is dishonest to say, as she repeatedly has said, that "Islam has nothing to do with terrorism." Islam has everything to do with terrorism. A solution can be found if the truth about the fundamental teachings of Islam is recognized, and then a reform movement within Islam takes place. Failing that, is America prepared to deal with eighteen thousand people who think that suicide bombings are often justified and another one hundred twenty-six thousand who think suicide bombings are sometimes justified?

What is being preached in America's mosques? Could it be the teachings of Islamic luminaries like Yusuf al-Qaradawi, the fiery spiritual spokesman behind the Muslim Brotherhood? On a religious talk show program on Al Jazeera TV called *Al-Sharia al-Hayat* (Sharia and Life), a question was put to Mr. al-Qaradawi: "Is it permissible—in the Syrian context—for an individual to blow himself up to target a group that owes allegiance to the Syrian regime, even if this causes casualties among civilians?"

Here is how he answered: "Generally individuals should fight and die in combat. However, if the need arises, **individuals should only blow themselves up if a group decides** that it is necessary for those individuals to blow themselves up. These are matters that are not to be left to individuals. Individuals should surrender themselves to the jamaa (the group), and it is the jamaa that determines how to utilize individuals according to its needs." (emphasis mine)

How wonderful! This is precisely the kind of teaching and advice that is illegal, not only in many countries but also under pertinent United Nations treaties. The UN's International Covenant on Civil and Political Rights (ICCPR) addresses itself to Freedom of Expression in its Articles 19 and 20. What does it say? Referring to Freedom of Expression it states that it "carries with it special duties and responsibilities." It echoes the Freedom of Speech laws in most countries that prohibit incitement to violence.

How many teachings that are like Mr. al-Qaradawi's are being preached in America's mosques? Are the same teachings being taught in America's Christian churches or synagogues? How long will this lawlessness be allowed to continue?

A final note on Mr. al-Qaradawi: he operates out of the Turkish city of Konya in central Anatolia. Konya is the Persian-Turkish name for Iconium, the ancient Greek city. The Apostle Paul preached and founded churches in Iconium during his first apostolic trip in AD 47-48.

Iconium then passed into Muslim hands when it was conquered by Arab Islamic armies in the eighth century. So, is Iconium part of the "native" lands of Islam, as the 1915 Ottoman Fatwa would claim, or is it part of the Christian native lands, which it was long before it was conquered by the forces of Islam?

And while we are on the subject of the "native lands" of Islam, we must ask ourselves: is Jerusalem itself part of those "native" lands of Islam? Why is Jerusalem said to be a holy city to Islam? It is not mentioned once in the Koran. Not only is it not mentioned in the contemporaneous notes from Mohammed's revelations of the Koran, but even the Caliph Osman, who as we saw earlier first put the Koran together in 650 AD—eighteen years after Mohammed's death—does not mention it in what became the Koran as we know it today. So how is it that Jerusalem is claimed to be a holy city for Islam? When Muslims kneel and pray five times per day, which city do they face? Mecca, not Jerusalem. Did Mohammed ever preach or teach in Jerusalem? No. Did the Israelite prophets of the Old Testament, and subsequently Jesus Christ, preach and teach there? Yes! The truth is that the only "relationship" between Islam and Jerusalem is by bloody conquest in the year 638 AD, when the Caliph Omar conquered it from the Byzantine Empire. And yet today, even under Israeli control, Jews are not allowed to openly pray on the Temple Mount hill in Jerusalem because Muslims have coerced them into not "defiling" Muslim holy ground with their prayers. Seriously?

We will close this chapter with some important and very telling statistics taken from authoritative sources, including The Pew Research Center, the World Public Opinion site, and BBC.

The Polling Company CSP (2015): Nineteen percent of Muslim Americans say that violence against Americans inside the U.S. is justified as part of the "global jihad."

ICM (2016): 2 in 3 Muslims in Britain would not report a terrorist plot to police.

Pew Research (2011): Only fifty-seven percent of Muslims worldwide disapprove of al-Qaeda. Only fifty-one percent disapprove of the Taliban.

BBC Radio (2015): Forty-five percent of British Muslims agree that clerics preaching violence against the West represent "mainstream Islam."

Pew Research (2011): Eight percent of Muslims in America believe that suicide bombings are often or sometimes justified.

Pew Research (2007): Twenty-six percent of young Muslims in America believe suicide bombings are justified; thirty-five percent in Britain; forty-two percent in France; twenty-two percent in Germany; twenty-nine percent in Spain.

Note: Please recall that the demographic for Muslims in the West leans heavily toward the under twenty-five age bracket.

European Values conduced a survey of Muslims living in Europe. It shows that forty-four percent of Muslims living in Europe have beliefs that correspond to fundamentalist Islam (https://stream.org/new-europe-survey-finds-44-muslims-believe-islamic-fundamentalism/). The survey defined "fundamentalism" for the ready reference of those surveyed as "a belief in returning to the roots of Islam, coupled with an adherence to a strict interpretation of the Quran." Seventy-two percent of the fundamentalist (the forty-four percent) also stated that they "would use violence to defend Islam." Of fundamentalists living in Germany, thirteen percent want to see Sharia as the supreme law; of fundamentalists living in Great Britain, sixty-nine percent want Sharia law, and of those living in France seventy-two percent.

These are shocking statistics that completely smash the delusion of European politicians that integration and assimilation of Muslim immigrant groups is taking place in their countries. Additional and disturbing statistics can be found at: www.thereligionofpeace.com.

Do many of our political leaders lack judgment altogether, or is it that they will say and sacrifice anything in pursuit of the "votes from the electoral margin" they court to secure their own election? Mainstream votes are now taken for granted. And most of our politicians, therefore, feel free to pursue those "votes from the margin" by parroting their message, because they can do so with impunity.

Churchill once observed that "democracy requires responsible citizenship.' Unfortunately, today our democratic institutions function with no responsibility and without accountability.

Many refer to ancient Athenian democracy whenever they wish to feel good about our political system. But Athenian democracy was not the same as what we have today. It was far wiser. First, government officials held office for only one year. Several times during that year they had to give account of their actions to the demos, i.e. their fellow citizens who could ask them questions directly and expected satisfactory answers. Second, they had a safety valve, a fail-safe mechanism. It was called "ostracism." Once a year, every voting citizen of Athens was issued an "ostrakon," which is a scallop shell. Inside the ostrakon they would write the name of one person in Athens whom they wished to ostracize. Whoever received the most votes was then ostracized. Ostracism meant that the person had to leave Athens the next day and not come back for ten years under penalty of death. That took care of cunning, plotting leaders of the demos who could wade their way through the demos' laws without getting apprehended. The public knew who they were, and the idea was that if the laws did not get them, for whatever reason, a simple plurality vote for ostracism would. How wonderful and wise! What better mechanism is there to keep officials and prominent people straight and sensitive to their fellow citizens? Can any of my readers think of a modern-day candidate for ostracism?

Which reminds me. In April 2005 I was in Havana, Cuba to co-chair a special session of an NGO I co-founded, the World Public Forum: "Dialogue of Civilizations." Fidel Castro had been requesting us to hold a session of the Forum in Havana for obvious reasons of prestige that it would bring to his country. My co-founder of the Forum, Vladimir Yakunin of Russia, who has served as President of Russia's largest company, the State Railways, agreed to Castro's request. We invited Fidel to address the Opening of the Forum, which included about 500 VIPs from more than sixty countries. His speaking slot was twenty minutes. He actually spoke to us for more than four hours. In his speech he referred with evident pride to ancient Athenian Democracy, its institutions, and how Cuba is now a true democracy. He then opened the Forum for questions. The first question that came to him was to define what Cuba's position is vis-a-vis terrorism. You see, Islamic terrorism was an issue of concern even then in 2005. He gave us, by my chronometer, a thirty-five minute reply to that question. It did not address the question. But he did tell us, with great flourish, that there are many who accused his government of torturing people in jail. And he ended by saying, "many are they who say we have tortured people in jail. So I will tell you, with full responsibility today, tortured we have none, executed by firing squad (fusillados), we have many." And he dismissively waived his left hand.

The author with Fidel Castro, Havana, 2005. Notice Fidel's left hand pointing to the author. Does not look like they were in agreement on much.

After that inspiring statement, I found a moment to be with him alone at the ensuing reception. I walked up to him and, taking license from the fact that I was there as a co-founder and co-chairman of the Forum, I placed my right arm around his neck, and put him in a mock "half-Nelson" lock. He was a little unsure of how to take this, but I was there with my very prominent Russian friend. His bodyguards took his cue and just looked on. Then I mentioned to him that as a Greek I was proud that he knew our ancient history and institutions of democracy so well. He replied "si, si" (yes, yes). I did not have the courage to ask him if he was also familiar with our institution of ostracism and to what degree it may apply to his person, but I did comment on how Athenian Democracy was all about human rights. He stared back at me through silted eyes conveying, I suppose, his puzzlement as to whether I was too stupid to realize what I was saying, or intentionally trying to insult him. I let go my half-Nelson and walked away smiling. I do not think he wonders to this day what I meant with that comment, but I do regret I did not bring up ostracism in such prestigious company. When I returned to the States, I received a phone call from my Russian co-founder. He said: "Nicholas, my colleagues and I are wondering: did you manage to make it safely out of Cuba?" I did, thanks to his presence there. I owe him one to this day.

PART TWO

THE U.S. CONSTITUTION AND OVERTHROW FROM WITHIN

"The United States SHALL GUARANTY
to every State in the Union a
Republican Form of government…"
(U. S. Constitution, Article 4, Section 4)
(caps are mine)

Allah is our objective, The Prophet is our
Leader, the Qur'an is our law, JIHAD IS OUR
WAY. Dying in the way of Allah is our highest
hope. Allahu akbar."
(The Motto of the Muslim Brotherhood)
(caps are mine)

WHICH SHALL IT BE, AMERICA?

Chapter 7

MUSLIM-AMERICAN CIVIC ORGANIZATIONS: THE DANGER FROM WITHIN?

Let us begin here with a very brief review of some of the most prominent Muslim-American civic organizations today. I am thinking of the Council on American Islamic Relations (CAIR), the Islamic Society of North America (ISNA), the Muslim Students' Association (MSA), to mention a few. In November 2008 in the Federal District Court of Dallas, TX the Holy Land Foundation (defendant in the case) was found guilty of the largest fundraising for terrorism case ever tried in a U.S. court. Holy Land Foundation had raised $12 million in the U.S. and then secretly funneled it to Hamas, an organization on the State Department official terrorist list. Federal Judge Solis, who presided over the trial, ordered that a list of three hundred and two Unindicted Co-Conspirators be published, signaling that American justice was telling the U.S. Department of Justice that these co-conspirators should also be tried for the same crime. On that list of three hundred and two, we find CAIR, ISNA, and the MSA as co-conspirators. Yet these organizations have regular access to the Obama White House and were never prosecuted by Obama's Department of Justice. In fact, in March 2010 Eric Holder, then the Attorney General of the U.S., circulated an internal memo advising that no prosecution of them would ensue.

Very prominent in the Muslim civic movement inside the United States is also a certain Mr. Abdurahman Alamoudi. He served as president of ISNA, among other prominent posts inside and outside our government. With his permission, I quote below a memo written by John Guandolo, former special agent of the FBI in counter-terrorism and presently founder of Understanding the Threat.

> "Abdurahman Alamoudi created and/or led two dozen of the largest Islamic organizations in North America, was a "Good Will Ambassador" for the U.S. Department of State, created the Muslim Chaplain program for the Department of Defense, worked with the Department of Education to determine what went into American public school texts discussing Islam, and met with U.S. leaders across the spectrum.
>
> "Alamoudi was arrested at London's Heathrow Airport in 2003 with $340,000 cash he got from the Libyan government for global jihad. He said he found it outside his hotel room. He was extradited to the eastern district of Virginia (Alexandria), where he pled guilty to an 18-count indictment.
>
> "The U.S. Treasury Department Press Release dated July 14, 2005 stated: 'In 2003, MIRA (Movement for

> Islamic Reform in Arabia) an al-Qaeda affiliate Saad al Faqih received approximately $1 million in funding through Abdurahman Alamoudi. According to information available to the U.S. Government, the September 2003 arrest of Alamoudi was a severe blow to al-Qaeda in the United States. In a 2004 plea agreement Alamoudi admitted to his role in an assassination plot targeting the Crown Prince of Saudi Arabia and is currently serving a twenty-three-year sentence.
>
> "Alamoudi was also caught on video in 1999 speaking adjacent to the White House grounds publicly declaring he is a fan of Hamas and Hezbollah—both designated terrorist organizations—to the loud cheer of the Muslims attending.
>
> "It should be noted that this behavior did not get him them fired from his positions inside the U.S. Government.

"Let's review: Abdurahman Alamoudi was the Islamic advisor to President Clinton and then went on to work with the Bush Administration. Alamoudi created the Muslim Chaplain Program at the DoD, worked as a Good Will Ambassador for the State Department, was widely recognized as a 'moderate Muslim', had unfettered access to the highest levels of power in our government, publicly pronounced his support for terrorist organizations and was an al-Qaeda financier who plotted with two U.K. based al-Qaeda operatives to kill Saudi Crown Prince Abdullah, who went on to become King Abdullah."

Note: The U.S. Government also considered Imam Anwar al-Awlaki a "moderate Muslim" and he gave presentations at the Pentagon and the U.S. Capitol, and worked with government officials. That lasted right up until he was killed by a U.S. drone strike in 2011.

In Appendix 1 of this book we supply a copy of an article by John Guandolo of Understanding the Threat, which we are reproducing with his permission. It includes photographs of Presidents Bush and Carter in the warm embrace of some f the leaders of Muslim-American civic organizations, including Alamoudi. All the Muslim leaders in those photographs head organizations that were determined to be Unindicted Co-conspirators in the 2008 Holy Land Foundation case, tried in the Federal District Court in Dallas, TX.

Many Muslim chaplains assigned by Alamoudi are still working with our military. They even set up the first mosque inside the U.S. Marine Corps, in Quantico, VA. Yes, yes, the same Marine Corps whose anthem starts with "From the halls of Montezuma, to the shores of Tripoli" in commemoration of the Marines' battles against the Barbary Coast Muslim pirates, who were based in Tripoli, Libya. Since Alamoudi's imprisonment, no one has checked the Muslim chaplains he put in place in our military for their loyalty to this Nation and to its Constitution.

Guandolo continues: "The numerous Islamic organizations Alamoudi created and led, and the individuals who worked with him providing material support to al-Qaeda, Hamas and the Muslim Brotherhood, can still be found walking the streets of Washington, D.C., the halls of Congress, working with the national security staffs, and elsewhere in America. "This dangerous pattern of our leaders and our media lifting up and proclaiming leaders in the Islamic community 'prominent moderate Muslims' continues today. Funny how far they all turn out to be terrorists."

WOW!

An additional comment is in order here: the total number of Muslims serving in the U.S. Armed Forces in 2014 has been estimated at about two thousand two hundred officers and personnel in all four service arms (Army, Navy, Air Force, Marines). Why was an extensive Muslim chaplains program even necessary, especially one initiated in 2003 (when there were even fewer Muslims in the Armed Forces) and one masterminded by Alamoudi?

Do the words from the "Explanatory Memorandum" we discussed earlier in this book ring true?

> "The Ikhwan (the MB fraternity) must understand that their work in America is a kind of a grand jihad in eliminating and destroying Western civilization from within and 'sabotaging' its miserable house by the hands of the believers so that it is eliminated and God's (Allah's) religion is made victorious over all religions."

They know what they are doing! Do we?

Let us now take a look at recent speeches made in public by some of the leaders of the great Muslim-American civic organizations:

> "We (U.S. Muslims) can never be full citizens of this country… because there is no way we can be fully committed to the institutions and ideologies of this country." Hassan Bagby, Advisory Board Member of ISNA in his

> keynote speech to ISNA Conference, Columbus, OH, August 2008.

> "Sharia law is above all man-made law."

Speech by imam al-Meneesy, President of the Islamic University of Minnesota, 2015.

> "If we are practicing Muslims, we are above the Law of the land."

Speech by Mustafa Carroll, Director of the Dallas Chapter of CAIR, at the Muslim Capitol Day rally in Austin, TX, March 3, 2013.

> "The work we should be doing is laying the Infrastructure—the administrative, logistical Infrastructure—putting that into place, so that if Allah puts us into a situation where we did have TO FIGHT, PHYSICALLY, we could translate that fighting into tangible political gains."

Imam Zaid Shakir, Lecture to San Francisco Bay area Muslims, first revealed in the book *Muslim Mafia*, by P. David Gaubatz, WND Books, 2009,page 259).

> "Christians are like feces and urine. They are the most evil of evils. Those who refuse to convert to Islam should have their lives and property taken."

Speech by imam Aby Ammaar Yasir Kazi, professor at Rhodes College, Memphis, TN, 2016.

Note: Can you believe that trusting parents are making sacrifices to pay their children's' tuition so that they can be taught this sort of stuff? For how long will we remain silent?

How have these people gotten away so far with saying such things, which are an incitement to violence and a call to overthrow the laws and government of the United States?

Are they using our laws of freedom of speech and freedom of religion to bring our nation and civilization down from within?

And if they are doing all of that, are they in fact violating existing U.S. laws that forbid such speech and activity? Are they not attempting to use our laws of freedom of religion and freedom of speech to bring down our "Republican form of government" provided in the Constitution, and impose in its place a barbaric dictatorship?

Here is what Title 18 U.S. Code, par. 2384 states on Sedition:

> "If two or more persons in a State or Territory, or in any place subject to the jurisdiction of the United States conspire to overthrow, put down, or to destroy by force the Government of the United States, or to levy war against them, or to oppose by force the authority thereof, or by force to prevent, hinder or delay the execution of any law of the United States, or by force to seize, take, or possess any property of the United States contrary to the authority thereof, they shall each be fined under this title or imprisoned not more than twenty years, or both."

What does this Title 18 mean when it refers to "any law of the United States" or to "the Government of the United States"? It means the laws and form of government that flow from the U.S. Constitution.

No person may conspire to overthrow the Constitution and laws of these United States. Period.

Therefore, Muslim civic leaders who are calling for activities that we see reflected in their speeches above are violating Title 18, par. 2384 of the U.S. Code. They must be indicted, tried, convicted, and sentenced.

It is the duty of every judge in the United States to uphold the Constitution and laws of this country. It is their duty therefore to implement Article 6 of the Constitution, which reads in part:

> "This Constitution, and the Laws of the United States which shall be made in Pursuance thereof; and all Treaties made, or which shall be made, under the Authority of the United States, shall be the supreme Law of the Land; and the Judges in every State shall be bound thereby, anything in the Constitution or Laws of any State to the Contrary notwithstanding."

Plainly speaking, the Federal and State Governments, as well as all judges, are bound to abide by and obey the U.S. Constitution.

Additionally, we have quoted as a heading to Part Two of this book, Article 4, Section 4 of the U.S. Constitution. Under this Article, the Federal Government is obliged to provide to every State in the Union "a Republican Form of Government." That does not mean government by the Republican Party; it means a form of government as provided in the Constitution. The now open preaching by civic leaders of

Muslim-American organizations calling for Muslims to see themselves as "above the laws of the land" and defying the laws and institutions of the United States of America threaten the absolute commitment and duty of the Federal Government to provide us all with a "Republican Form of Government."

The legal duty and right to prosecute those who conspire to do otherwise is clear and pressing.

Our choice is to continue to be the shining light to the world that we have been with guaranteed freedoms, God-given under our Judeo-Christian principles and written into our Constitution, or to become a banana republic.

What shall it be?

Chapter 8

THE UNITED NATIONS AND FELLOW TRAVELELRS OUTSIDE THE UNITED STATES

In Chapter 11 of my book *Islam vs. The United States*, we looked into the violations of the U.N. Charter (UNC), the Universal Declaration of Human Rights (UDHR, adopted in 1948) and several other major U.N. Treaties that are committed daily by the Organization of Islamic Conference (OIC). The OIC is the fifty-six nation (plus Palestine) international organization of Muslim majority nations. It daily violates the very Charters and Treaties of the U.N. that its member nations are treaty-bound to obey.

For example, the UDHR provides in its Article 18 as follows:

> "Everyone has the right to freedom of thought, conscience, and religion; this right includes freedom to change religion or belief..." And Article 3 of the UDHR reads I part as follows: Everyone has the right to life, liberty, and security of person."

The OIC member nations, after joining the U.N. and agreeing as a condition of membership in the U.N. that they would abide by these Treaties, did not feel inclined to obey what they had agreed to do.

So they met in Cairo in 1990 and issued The Cairo Declaration, which they then brought to the United Nations Secretary General. They then announced that they would abide by the Cairo Declaration. But does the Cairo Declaration differ in substantial ways from the UNC and the UDHR? Yes, it does.

For example, Article 3 of the UDHR gives everyone the right to life. But we know that Islam does not agree with this. Infidels do not really have the right to life, do they? Women who have brought "dishonor" upon the family do not have the right to live, do they? How does the Cairo Declaration handle these inconsistencies? Well, it speaks out of both sides of its mouth. The OIC Charter in its Chapter 1 (Objectives and Principles), Article 1, paragraph 7, states:

> "To reaffirm its support for the rights of peoples as stipulated in the U.N. Charter and international law."

Great!

The U.N. Charter grants equality to women, freedom to women, freedom of religion, and freedom of expression.

Now comes the double-talk: from the OIC Charter: Chapter 1, Article 1, paragraph 11 states:

> "To disseminate, promote AND PRESERVE (capitals are mine) the Islamic teachings and values based on moderation and tolerance, PROMOTE ISLAMIC CULTURE, and SAFEGUARD Islamic heritage."

What is that Islamic heritage exactly?

Is it not the suppression of women, their descent into second-class status, is it not killing the infidel, is it not honor killings?

The discrepancies between what Islamic nations undertook to abide by and what they actually do are laughable and tragic. And yet, the United Nations has let them get away with it. Which raises the obvious question: is the United Nations an honest organization, or is it the modern-day equivalent of the Tower of Babel?

Under the Cairo Declaration, killing is permitted if in Islam it is a "justified killing." It is justified if someone insults Islam. But it is most definitely NOT justified under the U.N. Charter.

With procedures and standards that are by now so corrupted from their original purpose and character, one has to seriously wonder if the United States ought to remain in the U.N. Plainly speaking, the present hypocrisy of the U.N. is unacceptable, and soiled the reputation and standards of the United States.

As if the above offenses were not enough, the United Nations Human Rights Council is now attempting to diminish free speech worldwide, and to redefine "hate speech" so as to protect and support Islam. In April 2011, when Madame Clinton was Secretary of State, the U.N. Human Rights Council pushed through, by voice acclamation, a new resolution known as Resolution 16/18. Prior to this resolution, hate speech, where it could be proven, came under civil laws on defamation. Resolution 16/18 now redefines hate speech as anything that incites another person to violence. Thus if a Christian happens to say to a Muslim that he believes in Jesus Christ and that incites the Muslim to violence, the Christian will be found to be guilty of hate speech. One can easily imagine that if this resolution is adopted by the

U.N. General Assembly, the word will quickly go out to Muslims to resort to violence at the slightest mention of Judaism or Christianity.

Who is behind Resolution 16/18? The OIC naturally, with the unholy and treacherous support of our then Secretary of State.

These are the sort of serious and dangerous developments that ought to be getting reported by our mainstream media, instead of what Ryan Lochte, our Olympic swimmer, did or did not do on the grass outside the locked restroom at the gas station in Rio de Janeiro. Nero gave Rome spectacles in the Colosseum, while the Empire was being usurped and destroyed. Who are the new Nero's?

The Resolution was put forward by Mr. E. Ihsanoglou of Turkey, Secretary General of the OIC, on April 12, 2011. This is the same OIC who, in the aftermath of the Charlie Hebdo issue that was "guest edited" by Mohammed, with the cartoon, issued the following statement:

> "Publication of the insulting cartoon... was an outrageous act of incitement and hatred and abuse of freedom of expression... The publishers and editors of the Charlie Hebdo magazine must assume full responsibility for their... incitement of religious intolerance."

After Resolution 16/18 was adopted, without an up-and-down vote by the Human Rights Council, Mr. Ihsanoglou had this to say about Madame Clinton: "I particularly appreciate the kind, personal interest of Secretary Clinton and the role played by the United States towards the consensual adoption of the resolution."

Certainly, Resolution 16/18 hides behind lofty language and high ideals. It begins by reaffirming everyone the right to freedom of religion, freedom of opinion and expression, condemns all acts of violence against persons on the basis of their religion, and then goes into "intolerance" of religion. Before we look at what it calls for, may we ask who is the most intolerant religion of all? Who forbids, under penalty of death, other religions to exist on their lands? And now that same group of murdering religious bigots step forward to invoke the West's freedom of religion foundations, with which to stanch any criticisms of Islam. If all this is not an exercise in surrealism, tragic surrealism, I do not know what is.

Having set us up with its lofty language, the Resolution then goes on to call on member nations of the U.N. to: Institute laws to "combat such incidents" of discrimination, hostility, and religious intolerance; adopt measures **to criminalize incitement to imminent violence based on religion.** (emphasis mine)

NOTE: OIC initiatives within the U.N. originally sought to make "defamation of Islam" a civil offense. Later this language was changed to "defamation of religion" and member nations were still called upon to institute civil defamation laws against it. Now the OIC has been emboldened enough, with the support of Hillary Clinton and the Obama Administration, to call for criminal laws against religious defamation (for which read "Islam").

In the process, free speech has been sent into exile by that supposed bastion of liberty, the United Nations.

The language of Resolution 16/18 is so lofty that if we did not know any better, it would be easy to fall for it. It goes without saying that Saudi Arabia, Pakistan, Qatar, and Afghanistan are not going to issue criminal laws to go after those who persecute Christians or Jews; only against those who dare to even criticize Islam. And it must be said that Madame Clinton, who issued a triumphal congratulatory message to the U.N. Human Rights Council on the day this Resolution was adopted, cannot possibly be thought to not understand that this is yet another effort by the forces of Islam to restrict freedom of speech in the name of freedom of speech. It is hard not to have utter contempt and question the motives of a U.S. Administration that aligns itself with such anti-Constitutional activity.

Let us make sure we understand the full implications of Resolution 16/18 if it's adopted by the U.N. General Assembly. In the massacre at San Bernardino, Mr. Farook, the great martyr for Allah, went to the county engineer's Christmas office party. While there, he got into a conversation with another employee, Nicholas Thalassinos, a Messianic Jew. Farook evidently was irritated that he was at an office party celebrating a Christian holiday. He exchanged some words, not in a fight or confrontation, with Mr. Thalassinos, who told him he was Christian and was enjoying the party. This irritated Mr. Farook enough to make him drive home, load up with his wife, come back to the party and kill fourteen people including Mr. Thalassinos. Were Resolution 16/18 to be adopted by the General Assembly and the U.S. to adopt new laws on hate speech per that Resolution, Mr. Thalassinos would be guilty of hate speech because he said something that incited another to violence.

Do we all understand the madness and Islamic dictatorship that is systematically being foisted on us?

What is taking place reminds me of a few choice words that Thomas Jefferson had for the U.S. Supreme Court. He wrote these words to an acquaintance, toward the end of his life, after he had done it all: written the Declaration of Independence, served as Ambassador and as Secretary of State, and then as President. Referring to the Supreme Court and its usurpation of power while everyone looked the other way (echoes of what Islam is doing today through "civilization jihad") he said:

"You seem... to consider judges as the ultimate arbiters of all Constitutional questions; a very dangerous doctrine indeed, and one which places us under the despotism of an oligarchy. The germ of the dissolution of our Federal Government is in the constitution of our Federal judiciary, an irresponsible body... working like gravity, by night and day, gaining a little today and a little tomorrow, and advancing its noiseless step like a thief, over the field of jurisdiction, until all shall be usurped from the States, and the government of all be consolidated into one."

I think of civilization jihad in the same terms: advancing its noiseless step like a thief in the night, while America sleeps and some of our politicians and mainstream media betray us.

As if the perils of Resolution 16/18 were not enough, another resolution is also pending before the U.N. General Assembly, Resolution A/HRC/22/L.40. It has gone virtually unreported by our media. It asserts that "terrorism... cannot and should not be associated with any religion, nationality, civilization, or ethnic group."

Really?

I do not see any Christians, or Jews, or Hindus, or Buddhists decapitating "infidels" with kitchen knives, putting them in a cage and immersing them into acid, crucifying them, etc.

Abraham Lincoln is credited with this famous aphorism: "You can fool some of the people all of the time, and all of the people some of the time, but you can't fool all of the people all of the time."

Chapter 9

FREE SPEECH IN AMERICA TODAY

We don't seem to be able to get it right these days. And yet it is not complicated to get it right.

Let's begin with what should be. That is the First Amendment. It reads as follows:

> "Congress shall make no law respecting an establishment of religion, or prohibiting the free exercise thereof; or abridging the freedom of speech, or of the press; or the right of the people peaceably to assemble, and to petition the government for a redress of grievances."

Generally, the legal record in America has protected free speech, except if it was an incitement to violence, or was treasonous or seditious. Period.

Justice Joseph Story, one of the Founders and of America's foremost jurists, states the following about free speech and the First Amendment in his *Commentaries on the Constitution of the United States*, written in 1833:

> "It is plain then, that the language of this Amendment imports no more than that every man shall have a right to speak, write and print his opinions upon any subject whatsoever, without any prior restraint, so always that he does not injure any other person in his rights, person, property or reputation; and so always that he does not disturb the public peace, OR ATTEMPT TO SUBVERT THE GOVERNMENT" (Caps are mine).

So what we have here from the inception of the First Amendment is the verbatim understanding of those who framed it, and not the subsequent sophistry of judicial activists who sat on the Supreme Court. We have here limits to free speech, clearly enunciated by Justice Story, such as no right to disturb the public peace, no right to defame another person, and no right to even attempt to subvert the Government of the United States. According to the above understanding of the First Amendment by one of the eminent Founders of our Republic and one of its original jurists, are not the speeches of Muslim-American civic leaders that we have quoted above attempts to subvert the Government of the United States?

Yet we seem to be living in in an inverted reality. The organs of our government and other important associations, instead of condemning the clearly subversive speech of Muslim-American civic leaders seem to condone it, while at the same time inventing new limits on free speech rights of Christians that have nothing to do with the Constitution.

As an example, I will cite the American Bar Association. That supposed bastion of protecting our Constitutional rights that regulates the nation's 1.2 million lawyers recently revised its *Model Rules of Professional Behavior* by adding a new rule known as 8.4(g). Why is what the ABA says in its *Model Rules* important? Because States have given the ABA power to accredit law schools and to lobby State courts into adopting its *Model Rules*. At its convention in San Francisco in August 2016, the ABA adopted this new rule 8.4(g), which severely encroaches on lawyers' right to freedom of speech. The rule says that it is "professional misconduct" to engage in discrimination "based on race, sex, religion, national origin, ethnicity, disability, age, sexual orientation, gender identity, marital status, or socioeconomic status in conduct related to the practice of law."

Seems innocuous, or well meaning enough, but let's scrutinize it. If a lawyer happens to express himself or herself as not admiring, for example, little rich kids, he or she risks suspension from the ABA or even disbarment. What if a lawyer says, "I dislike wealthy people, they ought to pay more tax"? Where does our Constitution make it an offense to comment on "socio-economic status"? The political correctness and self-righteousness behind this new rule is laid bare by the past president of the ABA, Paulette Brown, who said lawyers are "responsible for making our society better" and that because of the ABA's power, lawyers "are the standard by which all should aspire." What self-aggrandizement!

What happened to the U.S. Constitution and the standards it sets? And this megalomaniacal talk comes, no less, from a lawyer who ought to know better. Do we all see how politically correct activists are taking us farther and farther away from what the Constitution says?

At the same time, those who ought to know that they must watch what they say seem to be stepping over the line. Witness U.S. Supreme Court Associate Justice Ruth Ginsburg's recent debacle. In July 2016 she was interviewed twice, once by the *New York Times* and another time by CNN. During those interviews, she cast all the impartiality required of a Justice of the Supreme Court aside, and said that if Donald Trump was elected President, she "can't imagine what our country would be like" and that she might be inclined to follow her ex-husband's advice and move to New Zealand. By the way, I believe Trump might in such circumstances be inclined to say: "Great! I will pay for her ticket there!" Then on CNN she called Trump a "faker" and rhetorically asked, "how has he gotten away with not turning over his tax returns?" With such evident partisanship, how can Justice Ginsburg be relied upon to be impartial if, let us say, an election fraud case comes before the Court?

Justice Ginsburg (in a speech in South Africa) and Justice Breyer (in an appearance on the *Greta van Susteren Show* on Fox) have also said that we need to look to foreign laws for guidance, forgetting that their first and only duty is to uphold the U.S. Constitution. Such advocacy constitutes an impeachable offense for a Justice of the Supreme Court and warrants removal from office.

And let us not forget the exercise of free speech the Muslim-American civic leaders are engaged in, calling essentially for the overthrow of our laws and form of government, and the granting to only one religion, Islam, of ruling status above all other citizens.

So in these examples we have too much free speech, spoken irresponsibly. That is why I say we don't seem to be able to get it quite right, though doing so is really not that difficult. Laws already on our books make it easy to get this right.

In Part Three of this book, we will examine situations where our government and lawmakers got it right.

PART THREE

THE LIMITS ON FREEDOM OF SPEECH AND FREEDOM OF RELIGION IN THE U.S.

EXCERPT FROM A LANDMARK DECISON OF THE U.S. SUPREME COURT, 1931, in UNITED STATES v. MACINTOSH, WHICH MUST STILL INFORM AND GUIDE THE UNITED STATES:

"When he (Mr. Macintosh) speaks of putting his allegiance to the will of God above his allegiance to the government, it is evident, in the light of his entire statement, that he means to make his own interpretation of the will of God the decisive test which shall conclude the government and stay its hand. WE ARE A CHRISTIAN PEOPLE (Holy Trinity Church v. United States , 143 U.S. 457, 143 U.S. 470-471), according to one the equal right of religious freedom and acknowledging with reverence the duty of obedience to the will of God. But, also we are a nation with a duty to survive; a nation whose Constitution contemplates war as well as peace; whose government must go forward on the assumption, and safely can proceed upon no other, that UNQUALIFIED ALLEGIANCE TO THE NATION AND SUBMISSION AND ALLEGIANCE TO THE LAWS OF THE LAND, as well those made for war as those made for peace, are not inconsistent with the will of God."

283 U.S. 625, 1931 (Caps are mine.)

Chapter 10

A REVIEW OF OUR FIRST AMENDMENT FREEDOMS

The United States has faced, and faced down, past challenges to its freedoms guaranteed in the Constitution and to our form of government. Such challenges have fallen, principally, into one of four major categories:

a) Freedom of Religion, claiming rights antithetical to our laws
b) War and espionage (external and internal challenges)
c) Communism (internal and external challenges)
d) Freedom of Speech (internal challenges)

In all the above cases, the three branches of our government have managed to cooperate and agree upon a common policy, which was enacted by the legislative branch of our government, and subsequently supported by the judicial and the executive branches. There is every reason in the world to believe that once all branches of our government become convinced of the danger, they will once again cooperate in developing and enforcing laws that will safeguard the Republic. That is why it is so important to be able to clearly identify who, or what, the enemy is. Then, and only then, will effective measures be agreed upon to face down the particular challenges of that enemy. The majority of our political leaders so far have used all means at their disposal to deflect from the real issues, the real enemy. This is not unprecedented in our history, but it also has increased our losses of life and limb, until those political leaders could no longer ignore the reality of the challenge as well as those behind it. I believe that as the evidence unfolds of the true nature of Islam, not just "radical Islam" or "civilization jihad" but of what Islam really wants to achieve in the United States, recalcitrant political leaders will have no alternative but to acknowledge the obvious. But I grieve for those who will unnecessarily lose life or limb until our leaders can bring themselves to the right acknowledgment of who the enemy is. Until that time, permit me to bristle every time I hear the term "radical Islam" as opposed to "Islam." I repeat: there is no separate book of radical Islam. There is only one book of Islam and that is the Koran. Lastly, for those who will say, "You can't go to war with a whole religion," I would reply: "The choice is not yours. They have made it already. They are at war with us."

The governing principle behind all such efforts must always be our First Amendment. Since its adoption in 1791, the First Amendment has been through, or perhaps more appropriately suffered, differing interpretations that have at times limited or broadened its scope thanks to judicial interference with what is very clear language. And yet, it has to this day retained its main purpose: to protect and place limits on what is freedom or religion, freedom of speech, freedom of the press, and freedom of assembly and to petition our government for redress.

What fundamental characteristics does the First Amendment have?

First, it is directed at and to the Federal Government. It is addressed to what Congress may, or may not, do. Congress is the legislative branch of the Federal Government. It is not part of State government or Local government (townships, municipalities etc.)

Second, it prohibits the Federal Government from establishing a religion; there is no prohibition here of public prayer, or for allowing religious festivities. It is hard to see how, for example, public non-denominational prayer amounts to an "establishment of religion." And yet that is where our legal geniuses, judicial activists on the U.S. Supreme Court, have led us beginning with the Everson case in 1947. The result has been to push God out of America's public life. It's interpretation of "the free exercise of religion" is also what has led the Court to allow various religions, which at their core are against the American Republic, to continue their message. The Court, over a period of decades, has also seriously erred in extending to "non-religion," i.e., to atheists or enemies of faith, the same right that religion has. It is through this error that our government today is really an enemy of religion, which is a long way away from the Founders intention of only making certain that the Federal Government did not establish a national religion. Even liberal justices of the 20th century, such as William O. Douglas, who helped eliminate God from our public life and prayer from our schools, wrote in 1952 (Zorach v. Clauson) that, "We are a religious people whose institutions presuppose a Supreme Being." And yet, they went on to dismantle through a series of decisions the religious character of the Nation. It is hard to penetrate the mind of the judicial activist, led by lofty principles that invent, and destroys all in the name of intellectual perspicacity.

Third, the First Amendment prohibits Congress from "abridging the freedom of speech." There is no mention here of "free expression."

The Supreme Court has read into the First Amendment "freedom of speech" provision language that is just not there, namely "freedom of expression." It is the latter right that has led the Court to allow, for example, the burning of the U.S. flag, or the taking down of the U.S. flag in favor of the Mexican flag, or perhaps even the flag of ISIS. But the Constitution nowhere guarantees the freedom of expression. And just to be clear: it s not as though the Founders, who wrote the First Amendment, were inarticulate and not familiar with human "expression." They were. But they chose to protect freedom of speech, not freedom of expression.

Freedom of peaceful assembly was also to be protected. But is assembly peaceful when it advocates the overthrow of our laws, our Constitution, our Republic?

These are some of the topics we will explore in the chapters of Part Three, remembering that the liberal-progressive bloc has been steadily nourishing a monster: the freedom to destroy our freedom. Such a right does not exist in our Constitution.

Through all its mental gyrations, the Court has still left standing the fundamental protections built into the Constitution for the survival of our Republic. Let us recall, please, that Article 4, Section 4 still commits "The United States" to guarantee a "Republican form of Government" to the States in the Union. But, during the 20th century, the Court has taken on an increasingly liberal view, making "individual freedom" the new idol. This has been wrong, because the whole spirit of the Founders was for a unified Republic where rights were available, and limited, by the association of free persons who banded together for forming a Republic. In other words, the Founders' Republic was not meant to be a collection of egotistical individualists. The Republic had laws that were its bedrock, and those fundamentals were not to be changed except through a very onerous procedure of Amendment, requiring 2/3 of both Houses of Congress and ¾ of the State Legislatures. So, the 20th century phenomenon of the Court tilting dangerously toward a new idol, individual freedom, is not truly in character with what the Founders intended.

Why do I say this? Well, let us look at the very opening words of our Constitution. What does it say?

"We the People of the United States, in order to establish a more perfect Union...."

I do not see here any glorification, or even mention, of the individual. The spirit of the Constitution is, in fact, that of a *group* of people, who have God-given rights, getting together to establish a more perfect Union. The glory is first to God, and then to the Union of like-minded people. It is not to the individual. This liberal tilt of the U.S. Supreme Court toward glorifying individual freedom, even at the expense of the Union, is both legally and morally wrong. It is leading our country to disaster. It all began with Justices Oliver Wendell Holmes and Louis Brandeis in the 1920's.

We need to note here that the Founders' concept was based on Sir William Blackstone's principles, as laid out in his *Commentaries on the Laws of England*. In this book, he discusses the common law underpinnings of personal freedoms as compared to public order. In discussing freedom of the press and freedom of speech, he says:

"But to punish (as the law does at present) any dangerous or offensive writings, which, when published, shall on a fair and impartial trial be adjudged of a pernicious tendency, is necessary for the preservation of peace and good order, or government and religion, the only solid foundations of civil liberty."

The Founders who agreed upon the First Amendment, and in particular James Madison who is generally credited with writing it, all had in mind Blackstone's principles. They understood that individual freedom of speech and religion was being granted under the First Amendment, there were limits to the freedom of the individual, and those limits ended where the rights of the Union, or the Republic, began.

More than a century later, Justice Felix Frankfurter of the Supreme Court wrote confirmation of this principle in his 1951 commentary on the Supreme Court's decision in the Robertson v. Baldwin case in 1897. Frankfurter commented as follows:

> "The law is perfectly settled that the first ten amendments to the Constitution, commonly known as the Bill of Rights, were not intended to lay down any novel principles of government, but simply to embody certain guarantees and immunities which we had inherited from our English ancestors, and which had from time immemorial **been subject to certain well-recognized exceptions arising from the necessities of the case.** Incorporating these principles into the fundamental law there was no intention of disregarding the exceptions, which continued to be recognized as if they had been formally expressed." (emphasis mine)

His message, though wrapped in somewhat complicated language, is clear. The individual freedoms granted under the First Amendment are not a novel form of government. They merely are a recognition of ancestral English common laws. These exceptions, i.e. individual freedoms, however, have exceptions themselves, i.e. limits on those individual freedoms. What are those limits? When individual freedoms recognized under the First Amendment begin to trespass on the rights of the "more perfect Union," in other words, when those freedoms begin to threaten the very Republic.

If all this has been a little boring, I apologize to my readers. But it is necessary so we all better understand the philosophical underpinnings of our Republic and its laws. Also, so that we better understand what the intentions of the Founders were, and what they understood they were saying at the time they decreed it.

In other words, what did they mean when they said it? To answer that point better, we again go to Blackstone, whose principles informed and instructed the minds of our great early jurists, Founders like Madison, Jefferson, John Jay, George Mason, and Joseph Story.

Here is what Blackstone wrote in 1765: "The fairest and most rational method to interpret the will of the legislator is **by exploring his intentions at the time when the law was made**, by signs the most natural and probable. And these signs are either the words, the context, the subject matter, the effects and consequences, **or the spirit and reason of the law**." (emphasis mine)

Thus, and according to this simple principle, when the Founders stated in the First Amendment that "Congress shall make no law respecting an establishment of religion," they meant just that: Congress, i.e. the legislative branch of the Federal Government. They did not see the First Amendment as binding upon State government. And when they addressed themselves to freedom of speech, they meant speech, they did not mean "expression" as subsequent judicial activists on our Supreme Court have injected. What difference does the misinterpretations of the judicial activists make? An enormous difference, in overreaching the power of the Federal Government over the States, over our religious rights, and over giving license to those who want to tear down our Republic from the "more perfect Union" our Founders envisioned. For the last eight years we have borne witness to what happens when a Federal Government that overreaches and has not properly been kept in check under our Constitution, falls into suspect hands.

Among those who want to tear down this Republic and its Judeo-Christian foundations, which please remember can only be done with an Amendment to the Constitution requiring 2/3 of each House of Congress and ¾ of the State Legislatures; I count the forces of Islam.

Muslims should be acceptable into America if the religious and civic principles they espouse, and manifestly practice, coincide with our own. Continuing proof of that commitment may be necessary, as it has been of certain other religions whose principles were inimical with our laws. Mormonism, native Indian, and Shinto are precedent examples.

Freedom of religion and of speech are not license to tear down the "more perfect Union" that is our American Republic.

Chapter 11

IS FREEDOM OF RELIGION WITHOUT LIMITS?

INTRODUCTION

Under our Constitution and laws, is freedom of religion without limit? Can anyone preach and practice whatever beliefs or dogma they wish, and get away with it even if what they do is a violation of our laws and can even threaten the very existence of our constitutional Republic? Does a jihadi have the right to kill others while he screams "allahu akhbar" because this is an act encouraged in his or her religion? If he is prevented from killing, and locked up for life or sentenced to death, are his rights to free exercise of religion being violated? It is significant that at a number of trials for such murderers that they have put up this religious defense and told the court that they do not recognize its jurisdiction because this is God's (Allah's) law.

In a sense, bringing to trial a violent jihadi who has wantonly killed or maimed other people is easy. The violence is so abhorrent to us that we don't take any "religious" defense seriously.

But what happens if there is no killing, no violence? What happens if the proponent of whatever the questionable theory is, is peaceful while working to destroy our laws and our Republic? What happens if the perpetrator is a "civilization jihad" soldier? One who works constantly to undermine our laws and Constitution because that is his religious belief?

America has faced such peaceful, but ultimately destructive, soldiers for a cause before. They have come in the name of various causes: polygamy, refusal to provide medical treatment to a child because of religious beliefs, smoking health-damaging peyote and then claiming medical benefits from the state, communists, enemy supporters who spied on us in the cause of another religion or country, etc.

In the sections below, we will examine the historical and legal precedents that such cases have set, and then consider how those principles can be applied today to neutralize civilization jihad within the United States. And yes, we will discover that there are limits on freedom of religion that have been applied and used to prosecute and incarcerate past offenders.

POLYGAMY AND THE MORMON CHURCH

In 1878 the Supreme Court of the United States deliberated on and handed down a decision in the Reynolds vs. United States case. George Reynolds was a Mormon, living in the Utah Territory. He also served as Secretary to the President of the Church of Latter Day Saints (Mormons). He was married to Mary Ann Tuddenham when he willfully, and as an intended test of the U.S. Code, married Amelia Jane Schofield with a Mormon church officer presiding.

What was the law of the land at the time of his second marriage?

Section 5352 of the Revised Statutes enacted by Congress for the Territories of the United States stated:

> "Every person having a husband or wife living, who marries another, whether married or single, in a Territory of, or other place over which the United States has have exclusive jurisdiction, is guilty of bigamy, and shall be punished by a fine of not more than $500, and by imprisonment for a term of not more than five years."

Reynolds argued in his defense that in his religion it was an accepted doctrine of that church "that it was the duty of male members of said church, circumstances permitting, to practice polygamy... That this duty enjoined by different books which the members of said church believed to be of divine origin, and among others the Holy Bible, and also that the members of the church believed that the practice of polygamy was directly enjoined upon the male members thereof by the Almighty God, in a revelation to Joseph Smith."

So, much like Muslims today who claim they have a duty to jihad and conquest, Reynolds cast his breaking of the law as a religious duty.

In its unanimous decision, the Supreme Court said in part:

> "...the question is raised, whether religious belief can be accepted as a justification for an overt act made criminal by the law of the land. The inquiry is not as to the power of Congress to prescribe criminal laws for the Territories, but as to the guilt of one who knowingly violates a law which has been properly enacted, if he entertains a religious belief that the law is wrong."

And the Court went on, unanimously, to decide:

> "This being so, the only question which remains is, whether those who make polygamy a part of their religion are excepted from the operation of the statute. If they are, then those who do not make polygamy a part of their religious belief may be found guilty and punished, while those who do, must be acquitted and go free. This would be introducing a new element into criminal law. Laws are made for the government of actions, and while they cannot interfere with mere religious belief and opinions, they may with practices. Suppose one believed that human sacrifices were a necessary part of religious worship, would it be seriously contended that the civil government under which he lived could not interfere to prevent a sacrifice? So here as a law of the organization of society under the exclusive dominion of the United States, it is provided that plural marriages shall not be allowed. Can a man excuse his practices to the contrary because of his religious belief? **To permit this would be to make the professed doctrines of religious belief superior to the Law of the land**, and in effect to permit every citizen to become a law unto himself. Government would exist only in name under such circumstances." (emphasis mine)

This conclusive decision, and the principle behind it that the laws of the land when duly made by Congress shall govern over religious principle, remains to this day the foundation under the prohibition of polygamy in America.

By the way, how long will it be before the forces of civilization jihad demand, in addition to other licenses, the right to practice polygamy in the United States, since the Sunnah teach that the perfect man, Mohammed, practiced polygamy and even with underage girls?

Do we all see the wisdom of the Reynolds decision?

We shall also mention here a sequel to the Reynolds decision. In 1890 another case came before the U.S. Supreme Court, Davis v. Beason. The background of this case was an Idaho Territory Statute that made it illegal for a Mormon to advocate or encourage bigamy and polygamy. The Supreme Court unanimously upheld the Idaho Statute. Since bigamy and polygamy had already been found to be crimes in the earlier Reynolds case, the court now held that: "to teach, advise and counsel their practice is to aid in their commission, and such teaching and counseling are themselves criminal and proper subjects of punishment, as aiding and abetting crime are in all cases."

In other words, anyone who advocates breaking the law is committing a crime.

We shall see how far off this great principle subsequent decisions of the U.S. Supreme Court have come.

CHRISTIAN SCIENTISTS AND THE MEDICAL TREATMENT OF CHILDREN

Christian Scientists do not believe in medical treatment. Generally, they believe that is up to the Lord to cure the ailment or sickness of those who follow their denomination. When adults needing medical treatment are involved, the situation is clear. They are making an informed decision based on their religion and faith that they do not want medical treatment. It is their right. But what are the ethical standards that ought to apply in the case of minors—underage children who cannot make an informed faith-based decision on their own? Should their parents be legally allowed to refuse medical treatment, or even religious treatment such as healing?

Once again, what we have here is a legal dilemma between religion and our common laws protecting children. After decades of enacting State laws and after trial litigation, some of which reached the Supreme Court, standards have been imposed in almost all the States. These standards generally make it illegal for parents, in spite of their parental authority that is recognized in law, to forbid medical treatment for their children if their physical or mental well-being is under threat.

I am not aware of any uniform Federal standard of care for minors, as jurisdiction over such matters has mostly been left by the Supreme Court with the State Courts. Also the medical diagnosis and prognosis can be so different for each case that a uniform code has not been easy to establish. However, one fact is clear: as we look at the standards imposed by States on the parents, religious prohibitions on providing medical care to underage children have not been allowed. The American Medical Association and State laws have established the following general criteria for overriding religious belief with secular law.

If a child is in need of medical care, parents have leeway to make medical decisions provided those decisions do not endanger the life of the child. Many State Courts will allow their State Child Protection Agency to make a decision on medical treatment to be provided, regardless of religious belief, if:

a) The medical community is in agreement about the appropriate course of treatment for the child;

b) The expected outcome of that treatment is a relatively normal life with a reasonable good quality of life;
c) The child would die without the treatment, and
d) The parent is refusing consent for the treatment.

What the above means is that there must be agreement between the doctors that the contemplated procedure or treatment is likely to succeed, that it will not be destructive of the child, that if the child goes through the whole agony of the treatment, he or she will have the prospect of a normal and long life, etc.

As an example, we can cite a case that came before the Supreme Court of Delaware, Newmark v. Williams, where the parents objected to treatment because of religious beliefs and the State sided with them because the contemplated treatment was going to torture the child with only a forty percent chance of survival. A more recent case that came before the Court of Civil Appeals of Oklahoma, "In The Matter of D.R." the Court intervened to reverse the parents' decision not to seek further treatment of the child because of religious precepts and the chance of survival. The Court stated in its decision:

"It is well-settled that the State may order medical treatment for a non-life threatening condition, notwithstanding the objection of the parents on religious grounds, if the treatment will, in all likelihood, temporarily or permanently solve a substantial medical problem."

So here we see the State intervening, even in a non-life threatening case, to limit religious freedom if it contravenes our common laws about endangering the life of a child.

Generally, penalties for parents who refuse medical treatment of their child that the government has ordered, risk loss of custody of their child to the State.

This, therefore, is another example where the State takes precedence over religious belief, as it did in the polygamy case we examined above.

Chapter 12

FREEDOM OF RELIGION IN THE WORKPLACE

EMPLOYMENT DIVISION OF OREGON v. SMITH (494 U.S. 872, U.S. Supreme Court, 1989)

This would be a rather amusing case, were not important Constitutional principles behind it. It is a landmark case in establishing that freedom of religion has limits, even in times of peace, when religious practice infringes the common laws of our country. This principle has been trampled on by the Obama Administration in what we examined earlier in this book, namely the illegal and unconstitutional intervention of the EEOC (Equal Employment Opportunity Commission) in favor of Muslim truck drivers who refused to deliver alcoholic beverages. Certainly, it is to be hoped that the EEOC's action will be tested in Court and reversed. But we must note that it is typical of Mr. Obama, the self-styled Constitutional expert, that his Administration would use the EEOC to overrule the Constitutional precedent that the Oregon v. Smith case set.

What are the facts of this case? Messrs. Alfred Smith and his co-defendant Galen Black were working at an Oregon drug rehabilitation facility. They had ingested peyote, which they claimed was a religiously sanctioned practice of their church, the Native American Church. They were fired because they were "stoned" on the job.

They then sought unemployment benefits from the Oregon State Unemployment Division. It refused to pay such benefits because under its rules persons who had engaged in work-related "misconduct" were not eligible for unemployment benefits. They brought their case to the Oregon Court of Appeals, where they won. The Oregon Unemployment Division then appealed to the Oregon Supreme Court. It decided in their favor, holding that their religious right to peyote ingestion superceded the fact that peyote was a "controlled substance" under Oregon law. The Oregon Unemployment Division then appealed to the U.S. Supreme Court.

In 1987 the Supreme Court remanded the case back to the Oregon Supreme Court, instructing it to determine if a State prohibition of use of a controlled substance was a violation of Smith and Black's Free Exercise rights. The Oregon Supreme Court had not addressed this issue in its original decision.

On remand the Oregon Supreme Court decided that, yes, this was a violation of their freedom of religion rights. The Unemployment Division then again appealed to the U.S. Supreme Court, asking it to determine if this was a violation of Smith and Black's freedom of religion rights. The case thus came back to U.S. Supreme Court in 1989.

This time, the Supreme Court addressed the issue of religious freedom directly. In a 6-3 decision with Justice Scalia writing for the majority, it decided that Smith and Black's First Amendment rights had not been violated. The linchpin of this decision was that freedom of religion does not excuse a person from complying with a general law, duly enacted, that is not specifically aimed at religion.

Justice Scalia articulated this principle very eloquently, and also cited Justice Felix Frankfurter from an earlier (1940) decision. This is what Justice Scalia said: "We have never held that an individual's religious beliefs excuse him from compliance with an otherwise valid law prohibiting conduct that the State is free to regulate. On the contrary, the record of more than a century of our 'free exercise' jurisprudence contradicts that proposition."

He then quoted Justice Frankfurter from the Minersville v. Gobitz case (1940): "Conscientious scruples have not, in the course of the long struggle for religious toleration, relieved the individual from obedience to a general law not aimed at the promotion or restriction of religious beliefs. The mere possession of religious convictions which contradict the relevant concerns of a political society does not relieve the citizen from the discharge of political responsibilities."

And Frankfurter in that 1940 decision then went back to the Reynolds case (1878) that we examined above. He cited from that decision as follows: "Laws are made for the government of actions, and while they cannot interfere with mere religious BELIEF AND OPINIONS, they may with PRACTICES…" (caps are mine).

So here is another bedrock principle: religious freedom gives us the right to believe what we want, but that does not mean that we have the right to practice those beliefs if the practice contradicts our common laws.

Obama has got to know, even as a modest student of the Constitution, that the EEOC ruling on the Muslim truck drivers cannot stand up in court. But he has brazenly sought to make it the law, and cynically stands on the sidelines to see if the truck company will have the funds and patience to launch into a multi-year and very expensive legal battle. But I submit that ruling in this manner, Obama should be a prime candidate for the "ostracism" that the ancient Athenian Democracy practiced. His Administration's actions are an abuse of the system. And that is the TRUTH.

And to finish up with the Oregon v. Smith case: can we imagine so much money and talent wasted on two guys who just wanted to keep their jobs while they were stoned on peyote?

Chapter 13

JAPAN AND THE SHINTO RELIGION

We will now expand our historical and legal research into precedents of limiting freedom of religion from the intra-national, i.e., within the United States, to the international.

Those who know the history of World War II will recall Japan's role in starting the war with America in 1940. At the time, Japan had been under the control of the so-called War Party. This party had run the country for more than a decade and, building on the old Samurai ideology, had imposed a version of the Shinto religion called State Shinto on the country. Some of the basic tenets of Shinto were that the Japanese God was superior to all others, that their manifest destiny was to rule over other people and nations, and that they were the superior religion and race, etc.

Echoes of Islam?

This belief system led Japan to the war and to committing atrocities against the people of the countries it had conquered. Human medical experiments were conducted on Chinese people, the "rape of Manchuria" was extolled as proof of Shinto superiority, etc.

After the war ended in Europe with the complete surrender of the Nazis in early May 1945, the Allies convened in Potsdam, Germany to hold a conference on how to handle the ongoing war in the Pacific. Attending the Potsdam Conference were President Harry Truman, Prime Minister Winston Churchill (subsequently defeated in general elections and replaced by Clement Atlee by the time the Conference was over), and President Chiang Kai-Shek for China.

The Allies, addressing themselves to Japan, issued the Potsdam Declaration, from which we quote below. Articles 6 and 10 are truly historic because they represent a collective effort and determination of civil nations getting together to face down a militaristic-religious regime, define its destruction, and define its replacement with a liberal system of government based on Western principles. Indeed, as a student of history, I would argue that Japan has never known the prosperity and freedom it has enjoyed after the United States and its Allies took control over it in August 1945 and set limits to the religious teaching of Shinto.

Article 6 of the Potsdam Declaration reads as follows:

> There must be eliminated for all time the authority and influence of those who have deceived and misled the people of Japan into embarking on world conquest, for we insist that a new order of peace, security, and justice will be impossible until irresponsible militarism is driven from teh world. "

NOTE: What is Islam, with all its violence and pronouncements of imposing itself on all the world, its daily acts of coercion, bloodshed and terror, if not the modern-day equivalent of the "irresponsible militarism" referenced here by the Allies?

Article 10 of the Declaration reads as follows:

> "We do not intend that the Japanese will be enslaved as a race or destoryed as a nation, but stern justice shall be meted out to all war criminals, including those who have visited cruelties upon our prisoners. The Japanese Government shall remove all obstacles to the Revival and strengthening of democratic tendencies among the Japanese people. Freedom of speech, of religion, and of thought, as well as respect for the fundamental human rights shall be established."

NOTE: do these prescriptions sound like a good idea for application to what Islam is today?

What happened in the aftermath of the Potsdam Declaration? Two nuclear bombs were dropped on Japan in August 1945, which led to the Japanese surrender on September 7, 1945. The War Party protagonists, including the Prime Minister General Tojo, were tried and executed for their crimes. General Douglas MacArthur went into Japan in August 1945 as Supreme Allied Commander. He gave equality to women, created labor unions, restored peace and economic progress, and banned certain sections of the Shinto religion that had gotten Japan into so much cruelty and trouble. To those who today say that "nation building" does not work, look at Japan, look at South Korea, and look even at post World War II Germany. Those were all countries with no real democratic tradition. America gave those gifts to them. I do not say all this because I am a war-mongering "Neocon." I am not. Simply, I am an honest student of history who likes to speak the truth.

On December 15, 1945 General MacArthur issued "The Directive for the Disestablishment of State Shinto," generally known as "The Shinto Directive." It is historic in the benefits it brought Japan and in the precedent it sets for dealing with religions that are similarly militaristic to State Shinto. I say "benefits" because it freed the Japanese from the militaristic-religious code which had kept them as serfs in a feudal system well into the 20th century and allowed their society to evolve into a modern democracy with prosperity and common rights for all.

So what did the Shinto Directive say? Let us start with the preamble:

> "In order to free the Japanese people from direct or indirect compulsion to believe or profess to believe in a religion or cult officially designated by the state, and in order to lift from the Japanese people the burden of financial support of an ideology which has contributed to their war guilt, defeat, suffering, privation, and present deplorable condition, and in order to prevent recurrence of the perversion of Shinto theory and beliefs into militaristic and ultra-nationalistic propaganda designed to delude the Japanese people and lead then into wars of aggression, and in order to assist the Japanese people in a rededication of their national life to building a new Japan based upon ideals of perpetual peace and democracy…."

Breathtaking, isn't it?

It decisively addresses:

a) "Freeing" the Japanese people from "compulsion to believe in a religion or cult." Are Muslims compelled to stay in their religion, and are they under penalty of death if they choose to leave?
b) Lifting the compulsory financial burden off the Japanese supporting an ideology. Does this remind us of the compulsory "zakat" that every Muslim has to pay, amounting to ten percent of their income to support the needy (but actually very often used to support jihad in all its forms around the world)?
c) Lifting from the Japanese people the burden of their guilt in the war and their suffering as a result of their religion.
v) Do Muslims feel guilty for all the suffering their religion, which they financially support, imposes on the innocent victims of their terror? I would like to think so.
e) Preventing the recurrence of the "perversion of Shinto theory" into militaristic propaganda. Sound familiar in our present-day world with ISIS, and Al-Qaeda, Al-Nusra, and Al-Shabaab, etc.?
f) Rededicating their national life to a new Japan. Exactly what the Reform Islam voices, coming from within Islam, are demanding.
g) Perpetual peace and democracy. Could the Muslim world use a healthy dose of peace and democracy, so that the oppression may stop? Oppression of the masses living within Islam under corrupt governments, and oppression simultaneously of the Christian and "infidel" world from Islamic violence?

And what does the Shinto Directive order?

Paragraph 1(a): "The sponsorship, support, perpetuation, control, and dissemination of Shinto by the Japanese national, prefectural, and local governments, or by public officials, subordinates, and employees acting in their official capacity are prohibited, and will cease immediately."

Subsequent paragraphs of the Directive order that the State will cease immediately its support (financial and other) of Shinto, its teaching in public schools, the maintenance of Shinto shrines, the propagation of militaristic propaganda, school textbooks that teach Shinto, and the use of war-like or jingoistic language that refers to "the Greater East Asia War."

The Directive clearly states that there will be a separation of the State from Shinto. It also draws a distinction between "State Shinto" and "Shrine Shinto"—the latter being defined on the Directive as a non-belligerent religion that may continue in Japan but without State support.

Can we imagine a reform movement within Islam, or indeed, new U.S. legislation that would outlaw that part of Islam that teaches jihad, expansion, and violent take over of the infidel world? It seems to me that what the Supreme Allied Command fashioned for Japan in 1945 was a great compromise between that part of Shinto which was pure, non-violent religion, and that part which was militaristic and obnoxious to the rest of humanity.

Masterful!

A concluding comment on this. In the Shinto Directive we have the civil nations of the world, i.e., the Allies (The United States, Great Britain, Holland, France, Greece, Belgium, China, Indonesia, India, Iran, Saudi Arabia, Egypt, and many others) getting together to face down a world-menacing religious-military system. We have this movement led by personalities such as President Truman, Prime Ministers Churchill and Atlee, Chiang Kai-Shek, and others. If the principles behind the Shinto Directive were good enough for them, then they are good enough for me. And if they were good enough at that time, they are still good enough today. The civil nations of the world need to cooperate in facing Islam and those of its teachings that are militaristic and world conquering. The world does not need Islamic ideology to be saved. Rather, it needs to be saved from Islamic ideology as presently applied.

The Constitution of Japan, to this day, bars religion from controlling or influencing secular life. Article 14 of the Japanese Constitution states: "All of the people are equal under the law and there shall be no discrimination in political, economic, or social relations because of race, creed, sex, social status or family origin."

Their Constitution also bars Sharia or other foreign laws from being used in Japan, unlike England that now permits eighty-three Sharia law courts to operate on its territory. Article 20 of the Japanese Constitution reads: "No religious organization shall receive any privileges from the State, nor exercise any political authority. No person shall be compelled to take part in any religious acts, celebration, rite or practice. The State and its organs shall refrain from religious education or any other religious activity."

Let us try to put all this into perspective: an overwhelmingly religious state, dedicated to State Shinto and war-mongering against other nations and people because of its religion, was transformed in a short period of years, under Allied influence, into a non-religious state that foreswears the use of violence and the ideal of controlling and conquering others.

Let us hope and pray we see that same development occur with Islam. If it's achieved, Muslims will of course be free to worship their religion, but will no longer be free, or feel justified, in visiting barbarity and violence on the "infidel." Then, and only then, will they be able to live in peace with their fellow man. Then, and only then, will the prophecy given by the angel of the Lord to Hagar, the slave girl from Egypt with whom Abraham conceived Ishmael (the father of the Arab nations) perhaps be dispelled. In the Old Testament, specifically in Genesis 16:12, we find the Archangel Gabriel coming to Hagar and telling her:

> **"Behold you are with child and you shall bear a son. You shall call his name Ishmael. Because the Lord has heard your affliction, HE SHALL BE A WILD MAN; HIS HAND SHALL BE AGAINST EVERY MAN AND EVERY MAN'S HAND AGAINST HIM. And he shall dwell in the presence of all his brethren" (NKJV).** (Caps are mine)

Islam teaches that it is an Abrahamic religion, in other words a religion stemming from Abraham. Islam teaches that the Old Testament is divine revelation, though some of it may have become "corrupted." A question that comes to my mind is: what evidence does Islam offer that the Old Testament was "corrupted"? Do Islamic scholars have in their hands, for example, some ancient version of the Old Testament that dates to the year 1,440 BC (the approximate year when the Ten Commandments were given to Moses), which is contradicted by the version of the Old Testament that we have today, or by the version of the Torah that we have today? Or could it be the case that Mohammed had to claim that the Old Testament was "corrupted" because, while he realized he needed it as a platform for his new religion, he could not explain away its condemnation of Ishmael and his descendants? If Islamic scholars have such evidence of "corruption" of the Torah and/

or the Old Testament, I would love for the whole world to see it and for scholars to analyze it. Where is it?

In fact the opposite is true: scholars tell us, in a variety of books that have been written, that some of the oldest contemporaneous Koranic inscriptions that have been found, such as the ones written on the inside walls of the Temple Mount Mosque in Jerusalem (built around 640 AD), *do not match* their equivalent Koranic inscriptions that are put forward today. Who is addressing this issue in the Islamic world? What logical explanations for these differences have they produced?

Remember that in Christianity, as well as in Judaism, we have eyewitness accounts of miracles that God performed to show His glory. We have that evidence from contemporaneous accounts of those who witnessed the miracles. Where is the Islamic equivalent?

It may be important for Muslims to know what the Old Testament says about their ancestor Ishmael and his descendants. The Lord is very clear in Genesis (see Genesis 17:21 and 22:1-12) that His covenant is with Isaac, the child of His promise to Abraham, and not with Ishmael. I understand why the *Reliance of the Traveller*, and all Islamic teaching, forbids Muslims from studying other religions and even from discussing Islam itself for fear that such study may create confusion. When one reads what Genesis says about Ishmael and his descendants, we can perhaps understand why this prohibition of reading other religious texts exists in Islam. The religious teaching about Ishmael that we find in Genesis, which Islam confirms was divinely inspired, does not confuse Christians and Jews. They are free to read the truth in Genesis. It confuses, and keeps uninformed, only the Muslims.

The questions we raise here are not intended to show disrespect toward Muslims or toward Islam. They can believe what they wish, and we can believe what we wish. The trouble begins, and will escalate, when they seek to impose by violence and other illicit means their theology on Christians and Jews, and Hindus and Buddhists. Islam has got to come to terms with the fact that, today, Islam is always the instigator of this violent disrespect of others.

Chapter 14

LAWS ON FREEDOM OF SPEECH IN WAR AND PEACE

Since its inception, the United States has been at war many times. During some of the most challenging wars, internal as well as external challenges had to be met. In some of those wars, including the undeclared war with the French in 1798, The Civil War, World War I, World War II, and the Cold War, there was internal opposition and espionage that needed to be addressed by our government. Internal opposition was not always benign. At times it took the form of efforts to sabotage the people's morale, the morale of the Armed Forces, and incitement to violence against the war.

In all these cases, the First Amendment and Freedom of Speech notwithstanding, our government (legislative, executive, and judicial) took action to protect the Republic. Studying the history and judicial underpinnings of such actions provides a very important lesson on what can be done now to stop internal opposition to, and corruption of, our Republic by the forces of Islam. The legal and constitutional underpinnings of those earlier government actions can apply equally today. We will present them in the chronological order that they were enacted or adopted, together with a brief explanation of their history and effectiveness. What follows here does not attempt to be an exhaustive Constitutional analysis of each piece of legislation. Their very existence in our history, and a brief explanation of the rationale behind each, is sufficient. It proves the point we are attempting to make with this review.

A) THE SEDITION ACT OF 1798

> Officially known as The Alien and Sedition Act, this series of laws was passed by Federalist-controlled Congress and signed into law by President John Adams. These laws were opposed by the Democratic-Republicans (today's Democratic Party), led by Jefferson and Madison. They were thus not without controversy. The intent behind them was to control internal opposition and sabotage to the undeclared war against France, which was seizing U.S. ships on the high seas under the guise that the U.S. was siding with Great Britain in its war against the French Revolutionary government. The Sedition Act prohibited public opposition to the war. Fines and even imprisonment were called for against those who "write, print, utter or publish… any false, scandalous or malicious writing" against the government. In fact, twenty Republican editors of newspapers were arrested, as was a U.S. Congressman, Representative Matthew Lyon of Vermont. He was

jailed and actually re-elected to his seat while he was in jail. He was arrested because of his personal criticism of President Adams. The laws also provided for the deportation of foreigners, and set a minimum residence of fourteen years (instead of the previous five) for immigrants to have the right to vote. Jefferson and Madison lobbied the State legislatures of Virginia and Kentucky to declare the Sedition Act unenforceable within their States.

Fortunately, the war ended, and bruised feelings between America's top political leaders, Adams on the Federalist side, and Jefferson and Madison on the Democratic-Republican side, subsided. But these laws did set two important precedents: first that freedom of speech was not an unconditional right under the Constitution; and second that some States could de facto vote to ignore Federal legislation. That principle was later invoked by South Carolina at the time of the Civil War. Interestingly, Madison who at that time had been a strong proponent of Federal power, shifted to supporting States' rights. But during the undeclared war with France, the Nation did remain united against the enemy, and internal sabotaging of the war effort was stopped. Ultimately Jefferson and Adams did reconcile, and even died on the same day, July 4, 1825. Incredible, isn't it?

Moral of this story? Passions will flare up when such laws are contemplated or enacted, but if the common enemy is clearly identified, eyes will focus on the enemy and the Nation will pull together. And after the war, there will be internal reconciliation.

B) THE SEDITION ACT OF 1861

In the opening events of the Civil War, President Lincoln decided to suspend the Habeas Corpus provisions of the Constitution, first in the State of Maryland and in 1862 in all States. He did this in order to be able to arrest, and hold indefinitely, suspected spies for the Confederacy. In doing so, he ran straight into the opposition of the U.S. Supreme Court, which declared his actions unconstitutional.

It must be noted here that the Supreme Court at the time was packed with pro-slavery justices, who had declared in March 1857 in the famous Dred Scott case, that slavery was legal. Dred Scott was a slave who had escaped into a Free State and resided there for some time. Nonetheless, the Supreme Court decided he was not a free man. The Court went so far (can you imagine this?) as to say that African Americans could never be citizens of the United States. President Lincoln had openly defied the Dred Scott decision, announcing that he would not enforce it, and went so far to announce that any slave who escaped from his master and made it into Federal lands, including the District of Columbia, would immediately be given his freedom as well as a U.S passport. So defying the Supreme Court on its opposition to the Sedition Act of 1861 was relatively easy for President Lincoln.

What are the lessons we learn from this case? Once again, that imposition of such laws can be messy, with substantial internal opposition. Second, that somehow and in spite of sometimes legitimate criticism, God has protected America and the tactics of those of its leaders who had to take controversial action in the national interest.

So far, we have seen that both President Adams and President Lincoln ultimately were right in what they did, and are today considered heroes and not villains. It takes, however, courage to be a hero in the midst of a crisis.

C) THE SEDITION ACT OF 1918 – THE ESPIONAGE ACT OF 1917

The United States kept to its earlier principles of trying all it could to stay out of European wars. World War I started in August 1914, but the U.S. had managed to stay out of it until April 1917. However, in 1917, even under a liberal President, Woodrow Wilson, it had become impossible to ignore the war. American ships were being torpedoed by German submarines, including the famous Lusitania sinking. Additionally, in the spring of 1917, the Zimmerman Note came to light, demonstrating that Germany was conspiring with Mexico to from a wartime alliance. The confluence of all these events convinced both President Wilson and the U.S. Congress to enter the war. On April 2, 1917 the Congress voted for war. However, fifty Representatives and six Senators opposed the war resolution. They represented a substantial element that was opposed to the whole war effort.

President Wilson, I repeat a liberal, decided as every responsible leader must in time of war, that America's commitment required the whole nation to pull together with no internal dissension. The first piece of legislation toward achieving internal security and unity was the Espionage Act of 1917. Aiding the enemy, obstructing military recruitment, protesting conscription, and taking any action (oral or otherwise) to impede or criticize the war were made crimes, punishable by a maximum fine of $10,000 and twenty years in a Federal prison.

The following year, Congress also passed the Sedition Act of 1918, which broadened the Espionage Act. It made illegal any speech or activity that was disloyal to the U.S. Government, the military, or the Constitution.

The Act also prohibited the U.S Postal Service from processing and delivering mail that was critical of the war, or that obstructed its progress in any way.

Eugene Debs, the leader of the Socialist Party gave a speech criticizing the draft and praising efforts to obstruct war recruitment. He was arrested, tried under the Act, and convicted to ten years in jail. Hundreds of non-citizens, who were likewise critical of the war, were deported without trial. Approximately nine hundred people were tried and convicted under the Act.

The implementation of the Act led to several cases that were brought before the U.S. Supreme Court during and after World War I. Thus, in Masses Publishing Co. v. Patten (244 F 535, S.D.N.Y. 1917) the Court reviewed a decision by the lower Federal District Court in NY where the Postmaster of NY had refused to mail a publication titled *The Masses* that was critical of the war. The publication argued for disrupting the war effort. Justice Learned Hand wrote the majority decision, which found that the Postmaster had erroneously refused to mail the publication. What is interesting, however, is the principle that the majority decision of the Court enunciated with regard to First Amendment rights. It did not say they are absolute and inviolable. I quote here from Justice Hand's decision:

"One may not counsel or advise others to violate the law as it stands. Words are not only the keys to persuasion but the triggers of action, and those which have no purport but to counsel the violation of law cannot by any latitude of interpretation be a part of that public opinion which is the final source of government in a democratic state."

Justice Hand then went on to conclude: If a citizen "stops short of urging upon others that it is their duty or their interest to resist the law" then that person is still protected by the First Amendment.

So here we have the beginning of a legal differentiation between merely expressing an opinion, and calling to action against it.

Another significant case which stemmed from the Espionage Act that came before the Supreme Court was Abrams v. United States (549 U.S. 1145, 1919). Abrams and his group were immigrants from Russia and socialists. They were convicted of distributing pamphlets calling for general strikes at war material production facilities. It must be noted that in October 1917 the Bolsheviks had taken over Russia, and then made a peace treaty with Germany, the Treaty of Brest-Litovsk, in March 1918. The big Allies, Great Britain and the U.S., were contemplating sending their armies into Russia to bring down the Bolsheviks. Lenin and his agents in the U.S. wanted no one to go into Russia, so that Lenin could consolidate his control over the country. That is why Russian immigrants to the U.S., like Mr. Abrams, were now trying through propaganda to bring the U.S. war effort to its knees. They were trying to preserve the infant communist regime in Russia. Abrams was therefore acting as an international propagandist for the Bolsheviks when he began to drop his leaflets from the window of his building in New York, calling for general strikes to stop war material production. Abrams and his four accomplices were convicted under the Espionage Act. Interestingly, they had been in the U.S. for between five and ten years each, and had not even sought to obtain citizenship.

Note: Does this sound similar to some jihadis, who have come to the U.S. to agitate and attack our society from within, in order to help achieve the goals of international jihad?

The Abrams case came to the U.S. Supreme Court, where his defense was that preventing him from distributing the pamphlets was a violation of his free speech rights. It is hard to ignore the cynicism of a non-citizen, a communist propagandist, claiming as his defense the protection of the U.S. Constitution and his right to freedom of speech. Again, is there a modern equivalent to this, in Muslim Brotherhood front organizations whose agents operate in the U.S., with the intent to bring America down?

The Supreme Court upheld Abrams" conviction. The free speech protections he claimed were over fiery language in the two pamphlets he and his cohorts had been distributing, which included: "know, you lovers of freedom, that in order to save the Russian Revolution, we must keep the armies of the allied countries busy at home." In other words, he was advocating insurrection within the U.S. so as to keep our armies "busy at home."

Once again, the assumption that the First Amendment grants unlimited freedom of speech was shown to be wrong. And once again we see the precedent that once the Congress has identified the enemy and declared a condition of war, those First Amendment rights are adjusted to the level that our Founders *always* understood and accepted. It is only the liberal judicial activists of the 20th century who apparently have failed to understand that personal freedom is not the god of this Republic. The Republic was always meant to be a republic of "We The People." In other words, the people in their majority and seeking to have a "more perfect Union."

D) SCHENCK v. UNITED STATES (249 US 47, U.S. Supreme Court, 1919)

Charles Schenk was another communist agitator, who had published leaflets that he had mailed to draftees in the Armed Forces. In the leaflet he attacked the draft as a form of despotism, and called America's war against Germany a "capitalist war." His leaflets called for the repeal of the Conscription Act. He had been found guilty of violating the Espionage Act of 1917, and had appealed his conviction to the Supreme Court.

He lost. His conviction for violating the Espionage Act of 1917 was upheld. Justice Oliver Wendell Holmes wrote the decision for the majority.

The majority view was that Schenk's right to free speech did not protect him from his advocacy urging activities, which were unlawful under the Espionage Act.

But as with all decisions coming from the Supreme Court, great care has to be exercised in studying every word and principle that the justices put forward. That is where the potential for subsequent deviations from the Constitution will be found. On the face of it, the Schenck decision was gratifying to those who think that speech does not have unlimited rights. However, Justice Holmes interjected his judicial activism into the language of the First Amendment. Let us look at part of his opinion first:

"The question in every case is whether the words used are used in such circumstances and are of such a nature as to create a clear and present danger that they will bring about the substantive evils that Congress has the right to prevent."

Holmes' invention and injection into the First Amendment of "a clear and present danger" test, to define the limits of free speech, changed the landscape of free speech in America. After this decision, defense lawyers for others accused of violating the laws of the United States would argue that their clients' exercise of free speech did not present "a clear and present danger." Thus, if a revolutionary firebrand called for the demise of the Armed Forces, but did not incite his audience to immediate action, he was not violating the Holmes principle of "a clear and present danger."

E) FROHWERK v. UNITED STATES (249 US 204, U.S. Supreme Court, 1919)

A case similar to Schenck, but remarkable for what Justice Holmes said. Frohwerk was another socialist, who in 1915 authored a series of twelve editorials in a German-speaking newspaper, the *Missouri Staats Zeitung*, in Kansas City. The articles were against

America's involvement in the war. The trial court found him guilty of violating the Espionage Act. He appealed on the grounds that his free speech rights were being violated. The Supreme Court, in a unanimous decision, found that he had correctly been convicted. Justice Holmes, who a few months earlier had put forward the concept of "clear and present danger," wrote the majority decision and held that Frohwerk had engaged in a conspiracy. He stated that the First Amendment does not "give immunity for every possible use of language." Interesting concept, especially coming from a Justice who had just finished putting forward in the Schenck case the requirement that there must be a "clear and present danger" resulting from speech that violates the law.

F) GITLOW v. NEW YORK (268 US 652, U.S. Supreme Court, 1925)

Benjamin Gitlow was another communist agitator living in New York. He was tried in 1920 for violating a New York State law, the Criminal Anarchy Law of 1902. Gitlow had published an article titled "Left Wing Manifesto" in a newspaper of which he was business manager, *The Revolutionary Age*. Predictably, his defense argued that the article merely was a historical analysis rather than a call to arms. He was convicted of the charge, appealed to the NY Appeal Court, lost, and finally appealed to the U.S. Supreme Court. His appeal to the Supreme Court centered on his rights under the

14th Amendment, claiming that his right to "life, liberty and property" was being abridged and that his right to free speech under the First Amendment was being denied him.

As a very important point of law here we must mention that the 14th Amendment, adopted on July 9, 1868, was conceived as a protection to newly freed blacks in the Southern States. The 14th established, for the first time in U.S jurisprudence, two citizenships for every American: a Federal citizenship and a citizenship of the State in which that person resides. It then went to say that a U.S citizen's rights to "life, liberty and property" could not be violated by any State law without "due process of law." It was adopted to protect blacks who were still being denied their rights to property and to vote in the South, in spite of the emancipation the slaves won in the Civil War. It was, however, subsequently used in order to give extraneous rights to U.S. citizens that the framers of the 14th Amendment had not even thought of in their wildest imagination. Suffice it to say, that in June 2015 when the U.S. Supreme Court made its landmark decision in Obergefell v. Hodges legalizing gay marriage and imposing that legalization on the States, it used the 14th Amendment as justification. Clearly, the last thing that the framers of the 14th Amendment had in mind in 1868 was legalizing gay marriage. In Gitlow, the Supreme Court extended Federal law over the States with regard to freedom of speech, using the 14th Amendment as justification. In spite of this extension of the First Amendment freedom of speech protections on to State Courts, the Supreme Court upheld Gitlow's conviction 7-2, with Justices Holmes and Louis Brandeis in the minority. The majority, led by Justice Sanford, held that "the government may suppress or punish speech that directly advocates the unlawful overthrow of the government." Gitlow's original conviction of 5-10 years in jail was upheld, though New York Governor Al Smith later commuted his sentence to time served.

This case is a landmark for at least two reasons: first, that it upheld the government's right to limit speech when it calls for the overthrow of the government. Second, because the Court now had to take account of the "clear and present danger" criterion established by Holmes in the Schenck case. To do so, Justice Sanford, writing for the majority, relied on an earlier case, Shaffer v. United States (225 F. 886, U.S. Supreme Court, 1919) that had established an additional and useful criterion for judging the limits of free speech: the "bad tendency test." That opinion had stated that the "State may punish utterances endangering the foundation of government and threatening its overthrow by unlawful means." So Sanford set aside the "clear and present danger" test that Justice Holmes had invented, in favor of the principle that free speech does not cover speech that is intended to overthrow the government by unlawful means.

Sanford went further in his determination to try to extinguish the concept that Holmes had invented. He stated in his majority opinion that a "single revolutionary spark may kindle a fire that, smoldering for a time, may burst into a sweeping and destructive conflagration." This was his effort to set aside any requirement under Justice Holmes' "clear and present danger" test, that inflammatory, seditious and/or treasonous speech should first be evaluated for presenting any clear and present danger before the accused was found guilty under the Espionage Act.

The legal principles enunciated by Justice Sanford in the Gitlow case substantially apply to this day, and are directly pertinent to the advocacy of Muslim-American civic groups who want to impose Sharia law above the U.S. Constitution.

Holmes and Brandeis, writing for the minority in this case, still insisted, I think totally unrealistically, that no present danger existed in Gitlow's speech and activities because only a small group of people shares the views he had put forward in his manifesto. One thing about judicial activists is that they are both stubborn and arrogant. Can we imagine, for example, that Holmes did not already know that Russia had been taken over by a very small group of like-minded revolutionaries in the Bolshevik revolution? Yet, he was insisting, only eight years after Lenin's tiny band of thugs had forcefully taken over an enormous country, that Gitlow was not violating the Espionage Act because his was only a small group of people.

G) UNITED STATES v. MACINTOSH (283 U.S. 605, 607, U.S. Supreme Court, 1931)

Macintosh was a Canadian citizen and a professor living in the U.S. since 1916. He had applied for U.S. citizenship, but had made it clear in his application that he was not willing to bear arms in defense of the United States and/or its Constitution, except if he felt so moved in prayer to God. The Federal Court for the District of Connecticut had rejected his application for citizenship due to his statement above. In its decision, the Court had found that Macintosh was "not attached to the principles of the Constitution" which oblige all citizens to come to the common defense of the Nation. The Court reminded every one that the Naturalization Act required every applicant for citizenship to take an oath in open Court that he or she would defend the Constitution of the U.S.

The Court said that "Naturalization is a privilege, to be given, qualified, or withheld, as Congress may determine, and which the alien may claim as of right only upon compliance with the terms that Congress imposes." Further, it said "the common defense was one of the purposes for which the people ordained and established the Constitution."

The case eventually reached the U.S. Supreme Court. Macintosh lost. Justice Sutherland wrote the opinion for the majority. The Court went even further than the District Court had gone in its language of what privileges, and duties U.S. citizenship carries with it. It said:

"When he (Macintosh) speaks of putting his allegiance to the will of God, above his allegiance to the government, it is evident, in light of his entire statement, that he means to make his own interpretation of the will of God the decisive test which shall conclude the government and stay its hand. WE ARE A CHRISTIAN PEOPLE (Holy Trinity Church v. United States, 143 U.S. 457,143 U.S. 470-471), according to one another the equal right of religious freedom and acknowledging with reverence the duty of obedience to the will of God. But, also WE ARE A NATION WITH A DUTY TO SURVIVE; a nation whose Constitution contemplates war as well as peace; whose government must go forward upon the assumption, and safely can proceed upon no other, that unqualified allegiance to the nation, and SUBMSISION AND OBEDIENCE TO THE LAWS OF THE LAND, as well those made for war as those made for peace, are not inconsistent with the will of God." (caps are mine) 283 u.s. 625

What an eloquent and eternal expression from the Court. In one sentence the U.S. Supreme Court affirmed in 1931 the following:

a) That we are a Christian Nation,
b) That the Nation needs to survive, and
c) That the Nation's laws are not inconsistent with God's, and must be obeyed fully.

These three principles have not been reversed by the Court since 1931. Mr. Obama may have traveled abroad to announce to others, without any specific consent from the American people, that we are not a Christian nation any longer, but the authority of the Macintosh decision stands. And it also states that an individual's religious theories, likes and dislikes, of our laws and/or of our Constitution are immaterial.

The Court also affirmed that "It is not within the province of Courts to make bargains with those who seek naturalization. They must accept the grant and take the oath in accordance with the terms fixed by the law, or forego the privilege of citizenship. If one qualification of the law be allowed, the door is opened for others, with utter confusions as the probable result."

This decision also makes it clear that it is illegal to put ones allegiance to the will of God over his allegiance to the government.

Are Muslims who put Sharia law above the Constitution taking note?

H) THE FOREIGN AGENTS REGISTRATION ACT (1938) (22 U.S. Code, Section 611)

FARA was enacted by the Congress in 1938. It requires persons acting as agents for foreign principals in a political or quasi-political capacity to make regular disclosure of their relationship with the foreign principal as well as report on their activities and their receipts and disbursements in pursuit of those activities. The Attorney General of the United States has to report every six months to the Congress on the administration of FARA and the monitoring it provides of agents for foreign entities or governments. This report lists more than sixty countries that are monitored by the AG under FARA. A lot of the countries on the list are legitimate and allies of the United States. Others, like Russia or China are not necessarily.

The law requires that persons who represent "foreign principals," which includes foreign governments, government agencies (like a Tourist Board), foreign individuals, state-owned companies, opposition parties in other countries, airlines, etc., must register with the Department of Justice.

The law is far-reaching if it is properly applied. For example, a certain Mr. Khaled Abdel-Latif Dumeisi was arrested and charged with violating FARA because he was "acting as an unregistered agent of a foreign government." In his case he was supplying Saddam Hussein's government with information on political opponents who were in the U.S.

I propose that worldwide organizations, which are a threat to the United States like the Muslim Brotherhood, Hamas, and Hezbollah, must be on the list of monitored foreign entities. This would oblige Muslim civic organizations such as ISNA, CAIR, and the Muslim Students Association to disclose that they are agents for Hamas and the Muslim Brotherhood in the U.S., and to disclose the sources and destinations of their funding.

The law is on the books. Just use it!

I) KESSLER v. STRECKER (307 U.S 22, U.S Supreme Court, 1939)

This decision was based on the 1918 Sedition Act and further interpreted it. The 1918 law allowed for the deportation of any alien who advocates or teaches the violent overthrow of the U.S Government. It also provided that such aliens must be excluded from entry into the U.S.

The Kessler decision said that if any such alien had entered the U.S., being a member of such an organization or had after entry into the U.S. become a member, *but* had subsequently ceased being a member, then that person was no longer deportable.

J) THE SMITH ACT (1940) (18 U.S. Code, Section 2385)

Also known as "The Alien Registration Act of 1940." This law was enacted by the Congress on June 29, 1940, and has been amended and modified several times since then. Originally, it called for criminal penalties for advocating the overthrow of the U.S. Government and required all non-citizen adult residents in the U.S. to register with the government. About two hundred fifteen persons have been prosecuted under the Act, including communists, anarchists, and fascists.

The Act was sponsored by Representative Howard W. Smith, a Democrat. It was conceived as an urgent measure to confront two problems:

a) The sudden appearance of seditious "fifth column" people in other countries that were allies of the U.S. and which had suddenly been brought down by a combination of Nazi power and internal ("fifth column") sabotage. Characteristically, the House approved the Smith Act on June 22, 1940; the same day the French signed their surrender to Germany. The Senate did a quick voice vote approving the Bill, and sent it to Franklin Roosevelt who signed it into law on June 28, 1940.
b) Rising concern in State legislatures about the war and saboteurs within their State, which was about to lead to the adoption by many States of disparate and perhaps problematic local laws. So the Federal Government, represented by the Attorney General and J. Edgar Hoover of the FBI, stepped in to both

assure the States that it had the problem under control and to immediately adopt the Smith Act. Try to imagine a situation where, let us say, each State passed a different law without inter-State coordination, and the laws were conflicting. The Federal Government was right to take the initiative in this case.

The Smith Act had three Titles, or parts, to it:

1) Title 1 concerned subversive activities and called for penalties of up to twenty years against those who: "with intent to cause the overthrow of any such government (i.e. Federal or State), prints, publishes, edits, issues, circulates, sells, distributes, or publicly displays any written or printed matter advocating, advising, TEACHING THE DUTY, necessity, desirability, or propriety of overthrowing or destroying any government in the United States by force, OR ATTEMPTS to do so; or... organizes or helps or attempts to organize ANY SOCIETY, or ASSEMBLY OF PERSONS WHO TEACH, ADVOCATE, OR ENCOURAGE THE OVERTHROW OR DESTRUCTION OF ANY SUCH GOVERNMENT by force or violence; or becomes or IS A MEMBER OF, OR AFFILIATES WITH ANY SUCH SOCIETY,GROUP, OR ASSEMBLY OR PESONS, KNOWING THE PURPOSES THEREOF." (Caps are mine.)

NOTE: I have capitalized certain words in the Act. Let my readers ask themselves this important question: To what degree do the capitalized provisions, and the concepts behind them, apply to members of ISNA, CAIR, The Muslim Students Association, and any of the existing or future front organizations of Hamas and the Muslim Brotherhood? Like the "fifth columnists operating in the United States at the time of World War II, these front organizations for the Muslim Brotherhood seek the overthrow of the U.S Government and of State Governments.

Title I of the Smith Act made even "affiliation" with, and even "knowing the purposes" of, such groups illegal.

2) Title II of the Act dealt with deportation. The Smith Act modified that restriction imposed by the Supreme Court in Kessler v. Strecker, that if a person had ceased being a member of an organization which advocated or taught the violent overthrow of the Government he or she could not be deported. The Smith Act now stated that any person who "at the time of entering the United States, or... at any time thereafter" was a member of or affiliated with such an organization, was to be deported. Illegal weapons possession, or possession of heroin, or aiding illegal immigration were included in the category of violations that would lead to deportation.
3) Title III of the Act dealt with Alien Registration in the U.S. Anyone applying for a visa to the U.S. had t be fingerprinted and registered. Aliens (i.e. non-citizens) s who were already in the U.S. for more than thirty days and were over fourteen years of age likewise had to be registered and under oath also had to declare:

a) The date and place of their entry into the U.S.
b) Activities in which they had been, and intended to be, engaged in

c) The length of their stay in the U.S.
d) Their criminal record
e) Any additional declarations required by the Commissioner of Immigration of the U.S.

As a result of the Act, by January 1941 more than 4.7 million aliens who were in the United States had to register and be fingerprinted by December 26, 1940. The Act became law quickly, and just as quickly it was enforced! Imagine more than 4.7 million people having to register and be documented in a short span of six months. This is what the U.S. Government can do when it is not paralyzed by political correctness and has identified who the enemy is! The Immigration Division also started a successful campaign which showed that by registering and abiding by the law, registered aliens were "now safeguarded from bigoted persecution." Very soon after its adoption, the Act was expanded to include the alien's race, employer's name and address, organization memberships, and military service record in the U.S. or other countries.

Let us think about this: more than 4.7 million people were registered under the Act. Only those who were enemies of the U.S. had something to fear subsequent to registration. The overwhelming percentage of these people were in the U.S. for the right reasons. But those who were not, had been identified or, if they had avoided registration, were arrested and deported when found out. Is such a program of national security, of caring for America's own and true citizens, an abuse or a blessing? If it is an abuse, exactly whom is it abusing? And if it is a blessing, how many Americans does it bless and help protect?

Here are the facts: after the U.S. entered World War II in December 1941, 2,971 aliens (of the 4.7 million registered) were arrested. That group of 2,971 were enemy aliens and could have turned into the saboteurs or terrorists in our present-day equivalent. The rest of the 4.7 million continued to live safely in the United States. They were not trying to bring down our Government, and no one tried to bring them down. That is America. As the Bible says, "wise as a serpent, and gentle as a dove." This is what we need to be done again today in our problem with Islam in America.

We will now look at just one of the cases involving those other 2,971 who were taken into custody under the Smith Act. It provides a sound example of why such laws are necessary. In June 1941 the FBI raided the offices of the Socialist Workers Party in Minneapolis and St. Paul. The SWP was a Trotskyist group of the communist party that controlled Local 544 of the Teamsters Union. The SWP only had two thousand members all over the United Sates, but it had gotten to control Local 544! Local 544 had led a strike against the Works Progress Administration, an agency of the Federal Government, during time of war. That is sabotage.

Twenty-nine members of the SWP were indicted, arrested, and tried under the Sedition Act of 1861. Please think about this. In 1941, they were tried for violating the Sedition Act of 1861. This is what a national government does when it has properly identified the enemy: it uses laws already on its books, if they are sufficient, and enacts new laws where there are gaps. Why are we not doing this today?

The defendants were charged with having plotted to overthrow the government under the 1861 law, as well as under the Smith Act. During the trial, evidence was also introduced that the defendants had assembled a small arsenal of guns and pistols, had conducted target practices and drills, and had travelled to Mexico to meet with Trotsky. Does all this sound similar to arsenals being built by jihadis in the U.S. today, including "civilization jihadis"? Does traveling to Mexico to meet with Trotsky sound similar to jihadis from the U.S traveling to meet with ISIS and fiery imams in foreign countries who call America the "Great Satan" and openly call for its destruction? When are we going to wake up?

Of the twenty-nine indicted defendants, twenty-three were found guilty of various violations of the Smith Act, including attempting to overthrow the Government by force. They received 11-month to 16-month sentences. The punishment was not inhuman or excessive. In fact it was quite lenient. But the message to would-be troublemakers was being delivered. Do not plot against our form of government or you will be prosecuted, you will be tried and sentenced, and you will then be monitored for the rest of your life.

How many impressionable and immature Muslim youths in the U.S. today listen to the siren song of imams, both in U.S. mosques and ones abroad, and think they can become romantic "soldiers for Allah" with impunity? The threat of prosecution, destruction of name and reputation, conviction and sentencing, and jail time could well deliver a cold shower to such romantic delusions and help save American lives. Why are we not doing it? Is it because we still defer to the wishes of some of our political leaders who, in pursuit of a few more marginal votes that help only them, sell us the guilt-trip of "inclusion" and of "that is not who we are"? Do we really need Madame Clinton to identify for us who we are? Certainly, I would not wish to be who she is. And I do not wish to hear who she thinks I ought to be.

I will mention one more case that was brought to trial under the Smith Act in 1949. It is significant because World War II was now over, though America was now engaged in the Cold War and was seeking to protect itself from internal communist sympathizers. Ten leaders of the Communist Party were convicted under the Smith Act. They were sentenced to five years in jail and $10,000 fines. We will discuss this in more detail later in this book, as it became another landmark case (Dennis v. United States) after the U.S. Supreme Court confirmed their sentences in 1950.

K) THE McCARRAN INTERNAL SECURITY ACT of 1950 (also known as the Internal Security Act of 1950)

This act, introduced by Senator McCarran in 1950, is still U.S. law. Under the Act, communist organizations were obliged to register with the Attorney General, who in turn established the Subversive Activities Control Board to investigate people who were engaging in subversive activities or promoting the establishment of a "totalitarian dictatorship"—either fascist or communist.

NOTE: Doesn't Islam seek to establish a totalitarian theocratic dictatorship under Sharia law?

Under the Act, persons who were members of such groups could not become U.S. citizens, and existing U.S. citizens who were found to belong to such organizations could lose their citizenship within five years. The Act also provided for emergency detention of such persons and gave authority to the President to detain "each person as to whom there is a reasonable ground to believe that such person probably will engage in, or probably will conspire with others to engage in, acts of espionage or sabotage." It also allowed for the detention of "disloyal," dangerous, or subversive persons in times of war or of "internal security emergency."

NOTE: Do the leaders and members of such organizations as CAIR, ISNA, and their fellow travelers come under the definitions and provisions of this Act? Are they being "disloyal" to the United States and its Constitution when they call for Sharia law to overrule the U.S. Constitution? And are we now, as our leaders tell us, in a time of war against "terrorism" or not? So: if we are indeed in a time of war, and these people are being disloyal to the United States with their speeches, activities, conspiracies etc., can they be detained by the President under the authority given to him under the Act?

The Bill passed both chambers of the Congress and on September 22, 1950 was sent to President Truman for his signature. He vetoed it on September 22, 1950, sending it back to Congress with a note that he viewed it as "a mockery of the Bill of Rights." The House promptly overrode his veto by a vote of 286-48, and the Senate followed suit by a vote 57-10. I am an admirer of President Truman, but he was out of step with theinternal challenges facing the U.S. on this one. The support for overriding Truman's veto was heavily bi-partisan. Simply speaking, the Congress had had enough of the subversive activities of communists and their fellow travelers and was willing to stand up to a reluctant President in order to better secure and protect the citizens of this country. Do we see any echoes in this story to the present-day realities with the Obama Administration?

Various deportations and detentions took place under the provisions of the Act, but no one's constitutional rights to due process were violated. Senator McCarthy rose to prominence, not because of this Act but because of the general fear at the time of the "fifth column" that internal communism represented. McCarthy accused about two thousand two hundred people of being secret communists, but when his accusations could not be proven, the accused were set free. No system is perfect, and neither was the McCarran Act. But it did keep the Nation safe, and it did help deport a number of communists and fellow travelers. Some of the cases of those so accused under the Act came to the Supreme Court.

In Galvan v. Press (347 U.S. 522, U.S. Supreme Court, 1954) the Court upheld the deportation of Mr. Galvan. He was a Mexican citizen who had been residing in the U.S. since 1918. When he re-entered the U.S. in 1950 after a trip to Mexico, he admitted to the Immigration officer that he had been a member of the Mexican Communist Party from 1944 to 1946. Under the McCarran Act he was ordered deported. The Supreme Court affirmed his deportation. It also held that although Galvan may not have been aware of the Communist Party's advocacy of violent overthrow of the Government, it was enough that he had joined it of his own free will.

Additionally and very importantly, the Supreme Court settled with the Galvan decision another principle. Galvan's defense had claimed that Congress was bound to extend to aliens the right of "Due Process" specified in the 14th Amendment that all American citizens enjoy. The Supreme Court found that, no, Congress was not bound to extend substantive Due Process to aliens entering and/or remaining in the U.S. It also found that only Congress, and not the executive branch (i.e. the President) had authority to determine policies and the procedural safeguards that would apply. In short, aliens could not claim the same rights and exemption provided for in the Constitution to U.S. citizens, unless the Congress so decided.

Do we see how those powers vested in the Congress under the McCarran Act supersede, to this day, any extra protections for aliens who belong to disloyal organizations that the President may try to invent and impose? It is the Congress, and only the Congress, that has power over the admission of aliens and whether, and on what terms, they get to remain in the United States.

Some may argue that Senator Joseph McCarthy and the abuses of the Un-American Activities Committee that sought out communist sympathizers working in the Government, was a result of the McCarran Act. That is not so. McCarthy really rose to prominence after 1953. The Act had become law in 1950. No law is perfect, and urgent resistance to an internal and substantial threat is never perfect either. McCarthy did accuse some two thousand government employees of being communists; they lost their jobs, and were subsequently acquitted of the charges. That was wrong. But the McCarran Act and even McCarthy's committee also did a lot of good. And they created a climate in the U.S. that made it clear to those who were impressionable that playing with communism was not a good idea. McCarthy was discredited and lost his power in 1954. But the McCarran Act continued to operate and secure the U.S. internally. In fact it is a valid law to this day.

As the communist internal threat subsided, the Supreme Court began to scale back some of the powers given to the Government under the Act. So, for example, in 1965 in Albertson v. Subversive Activities Control Board, the Court invalidated the provision in the Act that obligated members of the Communist Party to register with the Government. It found this was a violation of their Fifth Amendment right against self-incrimination. The rationale was that by having to register as communists, they were incriminating themselves. And in 1967 in United States v. Robel, the Court decided that communists should not be prohibited from working for the Government, as this was a violation of their First Amendment right of Free Association.

But by 1967, the internal communist threat in the U.S. had almost disappeared. My conclusion is that the McCarran Act served its purpose well.

To come back to modern times, though communism shares some characteristics with jihad and Islam, the danger from the latter is much bigger. Why? Because Islam is a "whole life" system that covers religion, politics, the law, finances, and every aspect of life. And it is a totalitarian system that chops off people's limbs and heads. It is a system that enslaves women. Communism treated women as equals; not as property, not as sex slaves, and not as human beings with inferior legal rights to men.

The McCarran Act survives to this day as a valid legislation of the Federal Government. Various provisions of the U.S. criminal code, (Title 18) stem from the McCarran Act. Interestingly, it also provides for taking away U.S. citizenship from those who are found guilty of violating its conditions. I must emphasize this because we hear a lot nowadays about domestic-born jihadis who are U.S. citizens. Would letting it be known that such jihadis risk losing their citizenship perhaps make them rethink their ways?

L) PROCLAMATION 2914 – DECLARATION OF NATIONAL EMERGENCY BY PRESIDENT TRUMAN, December 16, 1950

In November 1950, just when the Supreme Allied Commander in Korea, General Douglas MacArthur, had declared that the offensive war against the North Korean communists had been won, hundreds of thousands of Chinese troops attacked the American lines and drove the Allies back. The Chinese attack was of such a massive scale that its repercussions were felt not only on the Korean battlefields but also all over the world. Suddenly, it had become clear to people of good faith like President Truman what communism was really about. So, only three months after he had unsuccessfully tried to veto the McCarran Act on September 22, he now issued Presidential Proclamation No. 2914.

What did the Proclamation say? Let us look at the opening recitals, which are always meant to set up the reasons for the Proclamation. Its third paragraph reads as follows:

"Whereas, if the goal of communist imperialism were to be achieved, the people of this country would no longer enjoy the full and rich life they have with God's help built for themselves and their children;

they would NO LONGER ENJOY THE BLESSINGS OF THE FREEDOM OF WORSHIPPING AS THEY SEVERALLY CHOOSE, the freedom of reading and listening to what they choose, the right of free speech including the right to criticize their Government, the right to choose those who conduct their Government, the right to engage freely in collective bargaining, the right to engage freely in their own business enterprise, and the many other freedoms and rights which are a part of our way of life; and..." (caps are mine).

Does the invocation by President Truman of the loss of freedom of worship remind us of what a victorious Islam would impose on America and Americans? Not to mention the loss of freedom for women, honor killings, forced marriages of underage girls, barbaric punishments that betray no social conscience (as for example when a little underprivileged boy steals and has his arm cut off as punishment)? What would President Truman think and do if he knew of the dangers Islam poses to the American Republic?

The Proclamation then went on to declare a State of Emergency and summoned all citizens, authorities (Federal, State and Local), industrial workers, and others to participate to the top of their ability in defeating the communist threat. It also called on all citizens to be loyal to the principles upon which the Nation had been built.

We need an equivalent declaration today, to summon the Nation to oppose and defeat the principles of Islam, which are antithetical to the founding principles of the American Republic. The constant support of the Left and of the Democratic Party for advocates of Islamic causes may well in time come to be viewed as treason to our Republic. Those who mindlessly parrot Islamic principles and give false assurances to the American public about how "terrorism has nothing to do with Islam" (as Madame Clinton has repeatedly stated), should realize that there may well be a day of reckoning for their disservice to the Nation and the American people. We need a modern-day equivalent proclamation to oppose Islamic teaching and objectives in the U.S.

M) THE COMMUNIST CONTROL ACT OF 1954

Congress went a step further than the McCarran Act in August 1954. Some critics have called The Communist Control Act of 1954 "anti-communist" hysteria. Typically, those critics did not live in that time. That was the time when the Soviet Union and the *Comintern* (Communist International) had declared that they were going to bring down the capitalist countries, with a particular emphasis on the United States. Why is it, by the way, that the enemies of freedom always want to bring the USA down? It was also the time when Julius and Ethel Rosenberg had helped deliver America's nuclear secrets away to the Soviet Union because they believed the world should be balanced in power and that it was immoral for the U.S. to be the only nuclear superpower. Let us also note that when the Communist Control Act was enacted by Congress in August 1954, Senator Joe McCarthy had already been discredited. The 1954 Act was not a hasty Act, or a witch hunt law. It had been carefully thought out and passed with strong bi-partisan support.

What did it specify? It stated: "The Communist Party of the United States, though purportedly a political party, is in fact an instrumentality of a conspiracy to overthrow the Government of the United States." And concluded: "The Communist Party should be outlawed." Any echoes here of what the Islamic movement in America is?

It therefore removed the "rights, privileges, and immunities attendant upon legal bodies created under the jurisdiction of the laws of the United States" from the Communist Party.

This law placed the Communist Party underground in the U.S. The Party did not disappear, but it was controlled, and ultimately not allowed to carry its strategy of bringing down the Government. The party still exists today and actually runs candidates in political contests. Critics will argue that the law was unsuccessful anyway, besides being unconstitutional, but that is the typical palaver from the Left. In a time of national emergency, the Party was declared illegal, it was controlled, its members were made subject to prosecution and in fact prosecuted, and their plans against American freedom and its Government were thwarted. Critics forget this part of the story.

Interestingly also, certain organizations that had been sympathetic to the Communist Party at the time, such as the ACLU, were also prosecuted under the 1954 Act. The ACLU had gained the dubious distinction from as early as the Gitlow case in 1925, of representing and defending known communists who were working to overthrow the U.S Government and Constitution. It had therefore come under the scrutiny of the Government.

I am not quite sure how the ACLU views with pride its role in supporting those who want to overturn our Constitution, and does so in the name of defending the Constitution. But then again, the twisted thinking of the Left never ceases to amaze, and appall me.

The 1954 Act survives to this day under 50 U.S Code Section 842, which states:

"The Communist Party of the United States, or any successors of such party regardless of the assumed name, WHOSE OBJECT OR PURPOSE IS TO OVERTHROW THE GOVERNMENT OF THE UNITED STATES, or the Government of any State, Territory, District, or possession thereof, or the government of any political subdivision therein by force and violence, are not entitled to any rights, privileges, and immunities attendant upon legal bodies created under the jurisdiction of the laws of the United States or any political subdivision thereof; and whatever rights, privileges, and immunities which have heretofore been granted to said party or any subsidiary organization by reason of the laws of the United States or any political subdivision thereof, are hereby terminated: Provided, however, that nothing in this Section shall be construed as amending the Internal Security Act of 1950, as amended (50 U.S. Code 781). (caps are mine)

So, what we have in this law is the outlawing of an organization, the Communist Party, because it sought the overthrow of the U.S. Government by force and violence.

Are many of the Muslim-American civic organizations seeking, perhaps, the same goal by similar means? Bob Gaubatz, in his very informative book *Muslim Mafia*, makes the point that this is exactly the goal the Council on American Islamic Relations (CAIR) has, and through violent means if necessary. For those who are not familiar with his story, he had his son pose as a Muslim diehard, who then worked inside CAIR for two years. He was an eyewitness to their secret planning, conspiracies, and methods of action. I recommend reading his book.

N) DENNIS v. UNITED STATES (341 U.S. 494, U.S. Supreme Court, 1951)

In 1949, eleven leaders of the Communist Party of the U.S., led by its General Secretary Eugene Dennis had been found guilty of violating the Smith Act for advocating the overthrow of the U.S. Government. They appealed their conviction to the 2nd Court of Appeals, and lost. They then petitioned the U.S. Supreme Court. The latter accepted to hear their appeal, but limited the scope of its review to the question of whether certain provisions of the Smith Act violated the First Amendment rights of the defendants.

The original trial, presided over by Judge Medina, had made quite a few headlines. The defendants had employed a three-pronged strategy:

a) To portray the Communist Party as a conventional political party which promoted socialist values. Aren't CAIR and ISNA engaging in the same dissimulation when they seek to present themselves as conventional "civic" organizations, while at the same time figuring prominently on the List of Unindicted Co-conspirators in the Holy Land Foundation case?
b) To portray the trial as a typical "capitalist" response to socialism, which could never provide a just result for "proletarian"

defendants. To this end, the defense made antagonistic and frequent motions and disrupted the proceedings in every way possible, so as to make it appear that justice was not going to prevail.

c) To create as much publicity as possible, through which to promote communist ideology.

Judge Medina, a former professor of law at Columbia University, would have none of this nonsense. He held the five defense lawyers in contempt of Court repeatedly, and had some of the defendants removed from his courtroom when they became rowdy and disruptive.

Note: does all of this sound similar to courtroom tactics that are often used by jihad defendants, who use the opportunity to scream that the Court has no jurisdiction over them, and that they answerable only to Allah?

The Supreme Court handed down a 6-2 decision, upholding the convictions of the eleven defendants. The Chief Justice, Fred M. Vinson (appointed by Harry Truman) wrote the decision for the majority, while Justices Hugo Black and William O. Douglas (both of Everson v. New Jersey Board of Education fame, or infamy) wrote the dissenting opinion.

The majority decision introduced a novel concept in confirming the defendants' conviction under the Smith Act: it went back to the concept first formulated by Justices

Holmes and Brandeis of "clear and present danger" and modified it to "clear and probable danger." Holmes' standard had not become the absolute standard when it was first promulgated in the 1920s, but now the concept was used in modified form to uphold Dennis' conviction. The Court cited the writings of Karl Marx, Stalin, and others to show that since those writings advocated the violent overthrow of capitalist governments, and since the defendants had been distributing and advocating those writings, there was "probable" cause of danger of overthrow. Justices Black and Douglas chose to posit that since the Communist Party was not really a power factor in America (a dangerous new concept, with no basis in the Constitution) and since they had not actually attempted to overthrow the Government by violence, their convictions should be overturned.

The Dennis decision definitely strengthened the hand of the Federal and State governments in facing down communist advocates. In essence, the Dennis case is remarkable because of its common sense. If you are advocating principles and writings that call for the violent overthrow of the Government and the destruction of the American Republic, you are engaging in an effort to overthrow the Government by violence. Lenin's grab of power in an enormous country, Russia, had demonstrated to all who have common sense that this is what communism is all about: the overthrow of capitalist governments through whatever means are possible, including violence, bluster, threats, and fear.

Does the Koran itself, with its call to violence, as well as the speeches of Muslim "civic" leaders in the U.S., also not meet the standard of probable danger?

As the internal communist threat subsided in America, subsequent Supreme Court decisions were handed down, which eroded the power of the Smith Act and the interpretations of it in precedent cases that had reached the Supreme Court (like Dennis). We will examine two of those case below.

In Yates v. United States (354 U.S.298, U.S. Supreme Court, 1957), the Court found that the Smith Act did not prohibit advocacy of the violent overthrow of the government "as an abstract doctrine." This is typical of the sophistry that the Court engages in, which is so exasperating to those who value common sense. So if, let us say, a college professor like Mr. Alinsky, advocates the violent overthrow of our Government but characterizes his advocacy as an "abstract doctrine," then it is OK? Did not Bolshevism take over and scar Russia, having started from the "abstract" teachings of Karl Marx and Engels?

Then in a further notable case in 1969, with Justice Hugo Black still serving on the Court, another decision was handed down in Brandenburg v. Ohio (395 U.S. 444, 1969). The Supremes further "interpreted" the Smith Act.

Now they held that "mere advocacy "of violence was, per se, protected under the First Amendment. Constitutionally unprotected speech, i.e. speech that was not protected under the First Amendment, was incitement to "imminent violence." Justice Jackson dissented, as he had in the Everson case. He clearly did not believe that the Republic had an obligation to shelter those who want to bring it down. He said:

"I find little indication that they (the Founders and authors of the First Amendment) foresaw a technique by which those liberties might be used to destroy themselves by immunizing a movement by a minority to impose upon the country an incompatible scheme of values which did not include political and civil liberties. The resort to that technique in this country, however fruitless, contemporaneously with the collapse or capture of free governments abroad, has stirred American anxieties deeply."

He was right, of course.

O) 8 U.S. CODE, Section 1182 (Enacted 1952)

This law was passed in 1952 and signed by President Harry Truman, a Democrat. It is valid to this day, and was used by various Presidents subsequent to Truman, including President Carter (another Democrat) who deported Iranians from the U.S.

The law is eighty-one pages long, so we will not analyze it in detail here. We will, instead, focus, on some of its key provisions. Inadmissible (and deportable) aliens into the United States, include:

Section 2 (I): aliens "who have engaged in moral turpitude." Polygamy is a moral turpitude under applicable U.S. law.

Section 2 (G): "foreign government officials who have committed particularly severe violations of religious freedom." That ought to include any government official from Sharia-law dominated countries.

Section 3 (A): "Any alien... who seeks to enter the United States to engage solely, principally or incidentally in... any activity (i) to violate any law of the United States relating to espionage or sabotage."

Section 3 (B) (II): any alien "who is engaged in OR IS LIKELY to engage after entry in any terrorist activity. (caps are mine)

Section 3 (B) (IV) (bb): "any alien who is a representative of a political, social, or other group that endorses or espouses terrorist activity." Does this include just about every practicing Muslim who takes the Koran at face value?

Section 3 (B) (VII): any alien "who endorses or espouses terrorist activity or persuades others to endorse or espouse terrorist activity or support a terrorist organization."

Section 3 (D) (I): "Any immigrant who is or has been a member of or affiliated with the Communist OR ANY OTHER TOTALITARIAN PARTY (or subdivision or affiliate thereof), domestic or foreign, is inadmissible." (caps are mine)

What is a "terrorist organization" under this law?

a) An officer, official, representative, or spokesman of the Palestine Liberation Organization (YES, Arafat's famous organization), and
b) Whatever other organizations are designated as terrorist from time to time by the U.S. Government (the list presently includes Hamas and Hezbollah).

What is "terrorist activity" under this law?

"As used in this chapter, the term 'terrorist activity' means any activity which is unlawful under the laws of the place where it is committed (OR WHICH WOULD BE UNLAWFUL UNDER THE LAWS OF THE UNITED STATESOR ANY STATE) and which involves any of the following: Hijacking, sabotage, seizing, detaining, threatening to kill another individual or compel a third person (including a governmental organization to do or abstain from doing any act as an explicit condition for the release of the individual seized or detained." (caps are mine)

NOTE: It seems to me that this section of the law automatically makes inadmissible into the U.S. any official of the Iranian government due to the recent "agreement" with it that involved the release of $1.7 million in cash to the Iranians and the simultaneous release of U.S. "prisoners" they held.

Chapter 15

THE LEGAL MEANS AVAILABLE TO THE U.S. GOVERNMENT WITH WHICH TO CONTROL ISLAM IN THE U.S.

In the previous chapter, we reviewed the existing legal means that the government has today, with which to oppose and control the forces of violent jihad and of civilization jihad. We will answer that question here, though I caution my readers that this is not an exhaustive list of laws which can be invoked for the purpose of protecting the U.S. and its citizens from jihadis and the supporters of Sharia law. Past legislation, or parts of past legislation, have since been revoked. For example, the Subversive Activities Board specified under the McCarran Act was revoked in 1973.

The point of citing all these past Acts and/or cases which came before the U.S. Supreme Court has been two-fold: first to show that there is a precedent for such legislation, designed to face down an internal threat to our form of government, and second to show that some part of these past laws are still valid today and can immediately be used to reign in the lawless advocacy against our government and Constitution that the Muslim Brotherhood front organizations in our country engage in.

If our government were to awake from the lethargy of political correctness into which our political leadership has thrust it, a comprehensive review of surviving laws ought to be undertaken, and then concerted legal action against the seditious speech and activities of jihadis in this country should be pursued. It is not hard to imagine, for example, a revived Subversive Activities Board that would prosecute advocacy of the overthrow of our Constitution and form of Government in favor of Sharia law. It is also not hard to imagine legislation that would shut down Muslim paramilitary camps, or government action that would immediately deport imams who advocate the overthrow of our laws or revoke the citizenship of jihadis. Finally, it is not hard to imagine a Federal Committee that would analyze the Koran and declare certain portions of it illegal in the United States, based on precedent cases limiting religious freedom and declaring some religious teaching, such as polygamy or Shinto, illegal.

Here is a summary of applicable laws that could be used or reviewed and strengthened against encroachment by Islam and in defense of our Constitution:

A) We still have the Smith Act, though somewhat weakened by the provision that advocating the overthrow of the government by violent means is illegal if it does not risk "imminent violence."

B) We have the McCarran Act, especially Title I of the Act, and the Subversive Activities Control Board that it established. The Board is to investigate persons suspected of engaging in subversive activities or otherwise establishing a "totalitarian dictatorship," which Islam on its face value certainly is.

C) 18 U.S. Code Section 2384 (The Seditious Conspiracy Law)
This law was enacted originally in 1940, and subsequently revised in 1956 and 1991. We will cite its full updated text here again for clarity's sake:
"If two or more persons in any State or Territory, or in any place subject to the jurisdiction of the United States, conspire to overthrow, put down, or to destroy by force the Government of the United States, or to levy war against them, or to oppose by force the authority thereof, or by force to prevent, hinder, or delay the execution of any law of the United States, or by force to seize, take, or possess any property of the United States contrary to the authority thereof, they shall be fined under this title or imprisoned not more than twenty years, or both."
NOTE: let us recall that the Muslim Brotherhood's manifesto, its Explanatory Memorandum, and the existence of twenty-two Muslim paramilitary camps in the United Sates, all testify to their willingness to use force to bring down the Government of the United States.

D) The First Amendment itself, which prohibits the establishment of religion, and thus would prevent Islam from being the religion of (or being supported in any way as a religion by) the Federal, and any State or Local Government in the United States.

E) The legal precedent set by the U.S. Supreme Court in its Macintosh decision in 1931. Aliens are obliged to obey all laws of the United States in order to become citizens, and cannot invoke their religious precepts above the laws of the land and the U.S. Constitution.

F) 8 U.S. Code, Section 1182 (The Inadmissible Aliens Law)

G) Those provisions of the Sedition Acts of 1798 and 1861, and similar laws to the present time, which are still valid.

H) New Executive Orders and Presidential Proclamations from the President, similar in concept to President Truman's Proclamation in December 1950.

Each and every one of the laws listed above can be very effective, if enforced, in stemming the tide of Islamic corruption of the principles and precepts of the American Republic.

PART FOUR

TOWARD A GRAND STRATEGY

Resurgent Islam poses a threat not only to the United Sates but in fact, to the whole world. Generally, it is acknowledged that the major power centers of the world are the European Union, Russia, The United States, China, India, and Latin America. A grand strategy designed to ally these major power centers to face down a resurgent Islam makes sense. In this chapter we will take a brief look at each of these centers of power with a focus on what the state of relations and/or threat is between each of them and Islam.

Chapter 16

THE EUROPEAN UNION

We have devoted a chapter of this book already to Europe's particular problems with domestic Muslim populations, as well as with newly arriving refugees. I am quite certain that, in spite of the stupid and politically correct verbiage that most European politicians engage in when talking about Islam and Muslims, in private they are keenly aware of the danger. In fact, I have had occasion to determine this through private conversations I have had with several Prime Ministers as well as Presidents of European countries. The EU needs to re-orient its policies toward immigration. Additional workers that it needs for its industry and to avoid declining populations due to low birth rates ought to come from Latin America, not from Muslim countries. Such a move would help stem not only the intrusion of more Muslim populations into Europe, but would also help stem illegal immigration into the United States. Imagine a situation where new European Union regulations allowed, for example, Mexicans, people from Central American countries, and even Argentinians to legally immigrate to the EU.

The U.S. has many alliances with European countries, beginning with NATO. What is needed now is a successful strategic alliance, not based on political correctness but real projections of what Europe may look like by the year 2050 with its ever-increasing Muslim population. If pragmatism prevails instead of the conundrums of liberal politics, concerted action between the U.S. and Europe can take place on fronts such as outlawing some of the teachings of Islam (as in the Potsdam Declaration in May 1945), and paring down the Muslim content of Europe through immigration from other Christian countries.

Chapter 17

RUSSIA

Russia has had an enormous problem with Islam for centuries, going back to 1242 AD, when Muslim Mongol armies established a kingdom in what is today the Kazan area in Tatarstan. Russia had become Orthodox Christian in the year 982 AD, when Tsar Vladimir of Kiev accepted the invitation of Emperor Basil II of Byzantium to convert his country to Christianity. At that time Moscow had not yet been founded, so the Russian Empire was a Kiev-based empire. After the 980s, Russia has had to repeatedly fight wars against the forces of Sunni Islam, especially in the Black Sea and Caucasus areas. During the three hundred years of the Romanov kings, repeated wars were fought between Russia and the claimant to the Muslim Caliphate, the Turks. It is interesting to note that the chapels located at Imperial Palaces, such as the Catherine Palace in Tsarskoye Selo outside St. Petersburg have an enormous gold cross on top of their cupolas, which pierces the half moon (symbol of Islam) at its foot. The symbolism of Christianity versus Islam is unmistakable.

Presently, Muslims make up a bit more than ten percent of the population of the Russian Federation. They are native born Muslims, not immigrants. Their birthrate is higher than the general population in Russia, and this creates a problem for ethnic Russians. At ten percent of the present population, Russia now has the highest percentage domestic Muslim population than any country in Europe. The state keeps strict control over any jihadi tendencies in its population and has come under repeated terrorist attacks. The taking of child hostages in Beslan (in the southern area of Dagestan) and of the wars in the late 1990s and early 2000s in Chechnya confirm that there is no love lost between Orthodox Russia and Islamic jihadis. We must note, however, that Russia's problem is with Sunni Islam. Shia Islam, whose leading protector nation is Iran, is a different story. Russia does not feel threatened by the distant Shia's, and therefore is more inclined to flirt with Shia nations. This may explain Russia's good relations with Iran, and with its proxies Hezbollah and the Assad regime in Syria. But Sunni Islam remains an open threat for ethnic Russians. As such, Russia has a continuing interest in keeping Sunni Islam under control. So do we. Terrorism inside America has all been Sunni-inspired. We have a problem with the Sunnis. Shia Iran may call us the "Great Satan" and call for our destruction, but the fact of the matter is that they have not attempted any act of terror on our shores. They have practiced terror against us on foreign lands like Lebanon through their proxies, but not on the American homeland. I submit that our problem with Sunni Islam is greater than our problem with the Shia's.

This makes Russia a natural ally for the United States and its expanding problem with Islam. However, since the fall of the Soviet State, the U.S. has missed golden opportunities to come closer with Russia. In fact, we have done the opposite. Here are six examples of our silly foreign policy toward Russia:

1) In 1999 we invaded Serbia, a historic and fellow Orthodox nation to Russia, to prop up Muslim Kosovo and Muslim Bosnia. Perhaps it would have been wiser for us to just insist that the Serbian strongman, Milosevic, be replaced. We had the power to do that, but instead sent in the First Armored Division and other elements of our Armed Forces, and came face-to-face with Russian troops that were there to protect their co-religionists. Not a smart move by the Clinton Administration.
2) In 2003 we invaded Iraq, a client State of Russia under Saddam Hussein. At the time, the trade relations between Russia and Iraq were strong. The top oil concessions in Iraq had been signed up by Russian oil companies like LUKOIL. After the U.S. invasion, these concessions were unilaterally cancelled by the U.S. and given instead to Western oil companies. This whole experience rubbed Russian pride by reminding them that weakness is victimization.
3) In the summer of 2008 we encouraged our protégé, President Saakashvili of Georgia to invade the borders of the Russian ethnic enclave in Abkhazia and South Ossetia. These regions were inside Georgia's borders, but were inhabited by ethnic Russians who are Russian and not Georgian. The President of Georgia sent in his army to impose closer control over the ethnic Russians. President Putin was obviously annoyed with this incursion and the upsetting of the delicate balance that had existed up until then. He felt compelled to intervene in favor of the ethnic Russians, especially since Saakashvili was engaging in adventures right on the Russian border. We must clarify that Saakashvili had lived all his life in Chicago until, with American support, he was sent to Georgia to run

for President. So in Russian eyes he was an agent of the U.S. An additional note is necessary here: Georgians have a generally very negative image among Russians. They are viewed as perpetual troublemakers from the days of the Empire. The fact that Stalin was an ethnic Georgian did not help their image among ethnic Russians. Nor did the fact that after the fall of the Soviet regime, the Georgian mafias ruled the big Russian cities abusing the local population. There was a saying at that time in Russia, which I am a witness to. Whenever an ethnic Russian saw a black limousine go by, which only the communist leaders had or the mafia bosses could afford, they would mutter "Limousin Gruzin" meaning Georgian limousine. Those words would be spoken with derision. And now, the Georgian army was entering the Russian enclaves within Georgia and strong-arming those minorities. For anyone who knew anything about Russia, Putin had no choice but to intervene. So the Russian army intervened by invading South Ossetia and routing the Georgian army within days. Such was the route that the Russian army could have taken, and kept, all of Georgia. It did not. Putin pulled it back, leaving only a small garrison to watch over the rights of the ethnic Russians in South Ossetia. And for his act of statesmanship and generosity in withdrawing the Russian army from Georgia, we call him a dictator. The Russian army intervention served to initiate in the U.S. all kinds of negative reporting on Putin. But, let's face it: major countries do not like games being played on their borders. That was the whole point of the Monroe Doctrine: serving notice on the British and on the Spanish empires that this *our* hemisphere. And that same doctrine was employed when the U.S. blockaded

Cuba in 1962 and told it that it could not have Soviet missiles. But in the summer of 2008, we were playing proxy games in Georgia, right on Russia's southern border. The Russian bear evidently was not pleased, and did something about it that we should have known we could not oppose. Silly tactics, that left another bitter taste in Russia's mouth.

4) In September 2008 our financial crisis and the mortgage-backed security scam caused a loss of more than $200 billion to Russia's Sovereign Fund. Their bright young men who were running the fund had invested heavily in our mortgage-backed securities. This was not a direct or premeditated act of hostility on our part, but once again it left a bitter taste in Russia's mouth. America was not to be trusted.

5) In 2005 the Bush Administration unilaterally withdrew from the Anti Ballistic Missile Treaty signed with the Soviet Union by Nixon in 1971. This was a Treaty of the United States, having been duly ratified by the U.S. Senate. Without deliberations with the Russians, we abrogated the treaty. And, having done so, we then announced that we were planning to install medium-range nuclear-capable missiles in Poland, a traditional enemy of Russia. For those not familiar with religion politics, Russia has always been Orthodox and Poland has been Catholic. In the 17th century, Catholic Poland had invaded and conquered Russian lands in the Ukraine. Eventually those lands were retaken by the Russians, but the enmity persisted. And now America was announcing within a short space of a few months a double whammy: cancelation of the ABM Treaty *and* installation of nuclear-capable missiles on Polish soil which threatened Russia once again right on its border. Why was this

necessary? The unilateral abrogation of the ABM Treaty served to create, yet again, inside Russia a conviction that the U.S. could not be trusted.

6) In February 2014, the U.S. announced through the statement of Victoria Nuland, Assistant Secretary of State for European and Eurasian Affairs, that the U.S. Government had "invested" $5 billion to bring down the democratically elected government of Viktor Yanukovych of the Ukraine. Since the fall of the Soviet empire, Ukraine had walked a very tight rope. It was trying to become a part of Europe and the EU, while at the same time not antagonizing its old master and historical sister, Russia. As we mentioned earlier, the origins of Christianity and of what is today Russia lie in the empire of Kiev. Ukrainians may speak a dialect of Russian, but historically Ukraine is to Russia what the New England States are to the United States. In the same way that much of our history, religion, and culture begin in New England, so do Russia's begin in the Ukraine. So, the presidency of Ukraine had delicately been alternating between a pro-Russian and a pro-Western president. Yanukovych happened to be pro-Russian. That did not by any means suggest he was going to detach his country from the West. There was too much aid money and cultural affinity between Ukraine and Europe for any such thing to be done.
Into that delicate mix jumped Mrs. Victoria Nuland and the Obama Administration. Not having properly learned lessons that they should have learned from their handling of Libya and the toppling of its government, they jumped into the Ukrainian adventure, once again

playing games right on Russia's border. What did Putin do as a first reaction?

Mysteriously, it became known that someone was systematically intercepting phone communications between Ms. Nuland and our Ambassador to Ukraine, Geoff Pyatt. During one such conversation before the Orange Revolution (which the Obama Administration orchestrated and supported), taped on February 7, 2014, Ms. Nuland is discussing with Ambassador Pyatt, who from among several Ukrainian politicians is best suited to be in the new government, the "revolutionary" government that they were planning to replace the democratically elected government of Mr. Yanukovych with. My theory is that Putin had this tape released in spite of thereby disclosing a major Russian intelligence breakthrough, as a warning to the U.S. to stop its plan. The Obama Administration chose not to take the hint. Yanukovych fell in the Orange Revolution, and a new pro-Western government was installed in the Ukraine. Two months later came Putin's reply: the annexation of Crimea. For those who may doubt this sequence of tempers and events, I ask a simple question: could Putin not have annexed Crimea earlier, was he so inclined? He has effectively been President of Russia since 2000. He could have invaded Crimea earlier. But he did not. He only did so after the American provocations in Ukraine. We hear much talk nowadays about the Russian "dictator." Even commentators, who should know better,

> like Charles Krauthammer, serially label Putin a dictator. Yet Putin is democratically elected. He has a four-year term under the Russian constitution. Democracy is not perfect in Russia. Then again where is it? But here is the problem: when our wise commentators resort to calling Putin a dictator, they steer attention away from another enormous Obama foreign policy blunder. It was Obama who lost the Crimea, not Putin who took it. The blunder gets pushed under the rug because Putin is the "dictator." And another problem: we tend to forget in America that Putin is President of Russia, not of the United States. His job is to serve Russia, not us. Our job should be to restore some good faith between our countries and forge an alliance that keeps the forces of Islam well under control. Are we too shallow to understand that?

Why have I listed the above mistakes in America's foreign policy? Because it hurts me to see how shortsighted we have been and how oblivious and lacking we are in having and executing an effective grand strategy against our biggest enemy, the enemy that will adversely influence the lives of our children and grandchildren, the historic foe: aggressive and violent Islam. Our first foreign wars were fought against Islam in 1804. Has anything changed?

If we want to restore relations with Russia, for our common good, we need to stop misrepresenting who they are. We need to stop insulting Putin, or his successor, labeling him a dictator. We need to show some respect. Let us not forget that there are those in America who consider Obama a dictator for the way he has ridden roughshod over the Constitution. We have a commonality of interests with Russia, ranging from Islam, to Syria, to nuclear non-proliferation, to trade. And let us not forget that Putin and his predecessor Medvedev have been doing a much better job than our President in supporting the family, Christianity, and in controlling Islam within their borders. For example, in order to reverse Russia's declining birthrates, which Putin inherited from the communist regime, the government there has a program of substantial outright monetary grants to families that have a second child, and more for a third, etc.

Putin also has actively supported Orthodox Christianity. I am an eyewitness to, and in a way a modest participant in, that. Every year in Jerusalem, at the Church of the Holy Sepulcher, a miracle takes place in front of one hundred thousand Christians on the afternoon of Good Saturday of the Orthodox Easter. The Greek Orthodox Patriarch of Jerusalem descends into the tiny chapel that was built over the temporary grave of Jesus, which lies under the roof and within the Church of the Holy Sepulcher. Before descending into this chapel, he undresses down to a simple tunic, and he is checked for any lighting material (matches, a lighter). Meantime the Israeli police allow, just on that one day of the year, one hundred thousand faithful to come into the church, most holding large unlit candles. During the service that follows, suddenly lightning-type flames strike the church, coming from above, running on the inside walls of the church, both vertically and horizontally, traveling through thin air, and hitting the roof of the tiny chapel over the grave. And people's unlit candles suddenly burst into flames. For the first three to four minutes the candle flame is white and does not burn. In fact, you see the faithful place their lit candles under their faces, bathing their faces in the Holy Light. About four minutes later, the candle flame turns yellow and burns. This miracle happened before my eyes, and I am an eyewitness to it. It happens every year at the time of the Orthodox Easter.

In 2004, Putin gave an instruction to my Co-Founder of the World Public Forum "Dialogue of Civilizations" Vladimir Yakunin to make arrangements to bring the Holy Light to Russia. I was called and asked if I knew of a way to transport the Holy Light from Jerusalem to Moscow. Immediately, my mind skipped to the Olympic Flame, given that 2004 was the year of the Athens Olympics. I called the Athens 2004 Committee to inquire how they transport the Olympic Flame from ancient Olympia (in the Peloponnese) to the capitals of the world. They advised me that they had seven very special lanterns, U.S. made, that they use to safely transport the flame. I asked if I could buy one or two. They said "no." I asked if I could borrow one or two. Again, they said "no." Finally I asked if they knew how I could get one. They told me that these flame containers were manufactured many years ago by a mining supplies company in the U.S., which had since gone out of business. A dead end. I then asked if they knew of anyone that might have some. They had an ancient list of overstock suppliers, which they very kindly shared with me. I hung up with them and called the first name on the list. It was a warehouse somewhere in the U.S. I had the exact model number, thanks to the Athens 2004 Committee. The rather sleepy salesman said he had two brand new ones in stock. I immediately gave my credit card and had them sent to me. Then I sent them to the office of my Co-Founder of the Forum, Mr. Yakunin.

The following year, on Good Saturday of Orthodox Easter in 2005, I decided to experience the appearance of the miracle of the Holy Light myself. A special Presidential flight arrived from Moscow to Tel Aviv, bearing Vladimir Yakunin, Russia's Minister of Culture, a couple of Archbishops, and other senior officials of the government.

They motored up to Jerusalem, attended the service at the Church of the Holy Sepulcher, and received the Holy Light. It was placed in the two containers I had found for them, put on the flight back, and arrived in Moscow by 11:00 PM local time on Saturday night.

Traffic had been closed off, and a motorcade was waiting for us. We drove straight to the Church of Christ The Savior on the edge of the Moscow Kremlin. This is a church that Stalin had dynamited and destroyed, and that Putin completed at a cost of more than $800 million. Assembled there was the leadership of Russia, waiting for the Holy Light to arrive and for the Service of the Resurrection to begin. As I looked around me, with Putin standing about thirty feet to my right, the Joint Chiefs of the Armed Forces, the entire Cabinet of Ministers and others. I realized this was the equivalent of being present at the State of the Union Address in Washington. Anyone who was anybody in Russia was there. The service started, went past midnight, when the Resurrection of Christ the Lord was celebrated, and went on and on (as Orthodox services are prone to do). Putin stood the whole time, reverential, moved, and humble. He did not leave until 2:15 AM. After the service, the Patriarch of Moscow, Alexy II, treated us all to a banquet in the vast basement of the church. There must have been several hundred people attending the Patriarchal dinner. I was thanked for having secured and donated the lanterns that carried the Holy Light. And I was happy that I was in a country that is not embarrassed by its Christianity. That is why I have relayed this entire story. Putin is no saint but, as a Christian, I have to ask myself: who does a better job of respecting and defending Christianity and the family? Putin or Obama? And who does a better job protecting his nation from dangers, foreign and domestic? Putin or Obama?

One more point here: as a Christian, I delight in the fact that Jesus manifests His presence through such miracles as I have described above and that I can see them and bear witness. How difficult it must be for those who seek God, and never have a confirmation of His favor and love through miracles that He shows them.

Chapter 18

THE PEOPLES' REPUBLIC OF CHINA

Islam allegedly first became known in China in 629 AD when an envoy of Mohammed, Wahab Abu Kabcha, arrived by ship in Canton. In 650 AD, the third Caliph, Osman, sent an envoy to Emperor Gaozong. But Islam did not take hold in China's east. It came in through its western provinces in Central Asia, where many Chinese are of Turkik origin.

Today, China has a serious problem with Islamic jihadis in its eastern provinces of Xinjiang (the largest of China's administrative regions), Shandong, and Qinghai. Part of the problem is that Xinjiang Province became part of China only in the 18th century and that prior to that it was a semi-independent state whose main population component was Muslim. After the collapse of the Soviet Union, pressure for autonomy emerged in Xinjiang, who considered that its Muslim roots entitled it to separation and statehood. Beijing, of course, would have none of this.

Tensions between Muslims and the Chinese government have been steadily rising since 2006. In the period leading up to the Beijing Olympics in 2008, the government began a serious crackdown on Islamists in the country. Then, beginning in 2009 a series of Islamic terrorist attacks occurred in China. In 2009 approximately two hundred people were killed in the regional capital, Urumqi, mostly Han Chinese who are disliked by the native Muslim Chinese. In June 2012 there was an attempted hijacking of a plane by ethnic Uighurs, a native Muslim group. In April and again in June 2013 police opened fire on Islamic demonstrators killing twenty-seven jihadis who were attacking police with knives. In October 2013 another car ran over a crowd in Beijing's Thiemann Square, and then burst into flames. In May 2014, jihadis crashed a car through a police barrier and tossed bombs into a crowd in the same province. Thirty-one people died, and more than ninety were injured. In April, July, and September 2014 there were more jihadi incidents in China, killing hundreds. Reporting on these incidents is not easy because the government restricts access by international journalists.

Finally, in mid-2015 the central government had had enough. It cracked down in the problematic provinces with a series of new and very restrictive laws against Islam. The government has blamed the East Turkestan Islamic Movement (ETIM) and its parent, the Turkestan Islamic Party, for the violence. It declared a "Year-long Campaign Against Terrorism," which includes laws that now forbid:

a) Praying in mosques;
b) Wearing of head-coverings by women;
c) Men from having long beards;
d) Men with long beards from riding public buses;
e) Islamic restaurants from not selling alcohol and tobacco;
f) Orders Islamic restaurants to display alcohol and tobacco in "eye-catching displays";
g) Orders Islamic restaurants to offer pork dishes;

h) Forbids government employees and their children from attending mosques;
i) Forbids people from publicly observing Ramadan, and civil servants from fasting during Ramadan;
j) And even puts Uighurs who do not smoke into a category that the government calls "a form of religious extremism."

Clearly the central government has gone on the offensive against jihadis and Islamists.

My point in reviewing all of this is that China has a serious problem with Islam. China is a natural ally in the fight against Islamic expansionism. What has the Obama Administration done about this obvious opportunity?

Additionally, the ever-present and ever-treacherous Mr. Erdogan, the President of Turkey, is trying to raise a "pan-turkik" identity and visited the eastern provinces of China in 2012 to promote this idea. He has not been invited back.

Chapter 19

INDIA

In 2004, at the World Public Forum "Dialogue of Civilizations," an NGO which I co-founded with Vladimir Yakunin of Russia and J.C. Kapur of India (www.wpfdc.org), we had among other guests Prime Minister Gujral of India as a speaker at the session held in Rhodes. Mr. Gujral opened his speech with a sentence that is etched in my mind. He said that he was addressing us as the representative of a country that is the largest democracy in the world and has the largest Muslim minority in the world (approximately 170 million Muslims). Most people think that after Pakistan and Bangladesh split from India at the time of independence, all Muslims left India to live in Pakistan or Bangladesh. Not so. Many Muslims remained in India, and today account for approximately 170 million people out of the total population of approximately 1.1 billion.

Mr. Gujral was speaking these words with a combination of pride and concern. Pride because there was no open fighting between Hindus and Muslims in India, but also concern knowing what a delicate situation exists. India is constantly at odds with neighboring Pakistan, especially over who ought to control the Indian Province of Kashmir.

There have been repeated incidents of Islamic terrorism in India, as with the attack on the luxury hotel in Bombay where jihadis hunted down room-by-room guests staying in the hotel, but those terrorists are said to have been from outside India.

The point here again is that India has a major potential problem. And having 170 million potential sympathizers in your midst is no easy matter.

Once again, I see alliance opportunities here. Possibilities for sharing intelligence, development of joint security programs, financial controls to stanch jihadi funding, and in fact to confiscate the resources of jihadi sympathizers.

Chapter 20
LATIN AMERICA

The general consensus is that there are about 4 million Muslims in Central and South America. Most reports state that approximately 700,000 live in Argentina, 1.5 million in Brazil, and the rest are spread between Salvador, Honduras, Venezuela, Chile, Trinidad, and Ecuador.

When does a Muslim presence begin in Latin America? It depends whose version of history you read. According to the website *Why Islam?,* Muslims explored South America long before Columbus "discovered" the Americas, and Islam was the second monotheistic religion introduced in post-Colombian America after Catholicism." The site then continues with the question in bold letters "Muslims in America Before Columbus?" and then comes a video speech by a certain Imam Khalid Griggs who asserts that Muslim explorers sailed from Spain to North America in the 889 AD, discovered it, and then sailed back to Spain. He refers to "documents" from their trip, without of course deigning to tell us where they are. When one watches such performances, it is hard to tell if one is watching a stand-up comedian from *Saturday Night Live*, or someone who should be taken seriously.

WHAT FACTS?

This is a laughable effort of the forces of Islam to once again inject themselves into Western history and to appropriate for themselves "facts" that are just not there. Nowhere on this site do they supply the "facts" they present in their text, such as dates of the exploration, the ships' names that did the "exploration," maps or records of the supposed exploration route, etc.

Additionally, and as usual with Islamic propaganda, they refer to themselves as the "second monotheistic religion" introduced to Latin America. Well, that is curious. Who is the first monotheistic religion introduced to Latin America then? The text implies it is Catholicism. Bit Catholicism, being a Christian faith, is not according to Mohammed a monotheistic religion. Recall that Islam, (see Sura 5 of the Koran) condemns Christianity for believing in the Holy Trinity. Islam teaches that there is only one god, and that Allah is not part of a Trinity. Do we all see how perpetually misleading the forces of Islam are? Why do they refer in this text to "monotheistic" religions? Because they try to curry favor that, after all, they are one of us. This is a dissimulation that is similar to what Muslims will tell Christians about Jesus. They will most often say, to surprised Christians, that Islam "honors" Jesus. What they will not say is that Jesus is only a prophet in Islam, not the Son of God, and they will also not say that Islam teaches that He was never crucified by the Jews and that He never rose from the dead.

But Islam is the master of dissimulation. Algebra, for example, was not invented by Islamic mathematicians. Some academicians say that the ancient Babylonians started it around 1900 BC, as evidenced by The Plimpton 322 tablet (dated to the period 1900-1600 BC) with a positional number system. The Egyptians and Greeks then developed more complicated algebraic equations that were not just linear like the Babylonians. The so-called Rhind Papyrus dated to 1650 BC shows the development of Egyptian algebraic thinking. The Greek mathematician, Pythagoras, did his part too around 520 BC teaching philosophy and math (and what is now called algebra) in Samos and also at the academy he founded in what is today Crotone, Italy. Another group of academicians say that the "father of algebra" in the sense that algebra is a theory of equations, was the Greek mathematician Diophantus, who taught around 150 BC. Definitely, however, it was *not* Muslim mathematicians that invented it, as Islam does not even appear on the world map until 622 AD. But, no matter, Islamic propaganda has it that in spite of all this historic evidence, Islamic mathematicians invented algebra, simply because the name algebra derives from the Arabic "al-jabr" which means "reunion of broken parts." They claim that a Persian mathematician, al-Khwarizmi, who lived in 850 AD (i.e. 2,750 years after the Babylonian invention of algebra) invented it. How do they get away with this kind of stuff? And how long must the rest of humanity put up with all the dissimulation, trying not to "offend" anyone? Islamic dissimulation on all fronts, religious, scientific, ethical, historical?

Now back to Latin America. Shia jihadis were the first to make Islam's benevolent presence felt in Latin America, when in 1992 they bombed the Israeli Embassy in Buenos Aires, Argentina. They killed twenty-nine and injured more than two hundred fifty innocents in that heroic engagement. Then in 1994, Iran's proxy Hezbollah bombed AMIA, a Jewish community center in Buenos Aires, this time killing eighty-seven and injuring another one hundred people. When Hugo Chavez rose to power in Venezuela, he struck up close relations with Iran's President Mahmoud Ahmadinejad. As a result of that friendship,

Hezbollah's two networks, the Rabbani network and the Nasseredine network established more than eighty "cultural centers" in Latin America. Today, there is very serious concern that these networks which have been training young jihadis coming in from the Middle East and also domestically procured, will launch terrorist acts in the United States. Imagine how easy this is. No border controls, no wall.

Sunni Islam has been playing catch-up to the Shia presence in Latin America. But those numbers are now increasing too. For example, the origins of the five jihadis arrested in Honduras last November with fake Greek passports that we mentioned earlier in the book are impossible to determine. When they were arrested because they could not speak Greek, they said they were "students." No doubt. Students of everything that is barbaric, ungodly, and deadly. What a shame if these young men really are "god-seekers" who have been steered wrong by their imams....

U.S. counter-terrorism experts state that they consider an attack in the homeland that originates from jihadi sleeper cells already based in Latin America "highly likely."

In reviewing the jihad presence in Latin America, which has historically been strongly Catholic, it is inconceivable that valuable alliances cannot be struck up between the United States and at least some of the more important Latin American states which do not welcome the prospect of violent sleeper cells in their midst. The argument here is that these sleeper cells may be directed against the U.S., but really they are directed at all infidels. So, at least some of the Latin nations have got to be interested in cooperating with the U.S. in eliminating such dangers. And those Latin nations that do not will have hell to pay for their mistakes. That much is certain.

In summary: the United Sates can pursue new international alliances with each and every country or nation group that we have examined in this Part Four, in implementing an anti-terror and anti-jihadi strategy. Old alliances and old enmities must be swept aside in the face of this clear and present danger.

The cooperation opportunities are endless and pressing. Islam has managed to make itself, through its civilization jihadis, through its terrorists, and through the fellow travelers of the jihadis, a major problem for the world's peace-loving people.

PART FIVE

SOME CONCLUSIONS

Chapter 21

A PRELIMINARY PLAN

We do not pretend to offer here a comprehensive plan of action. What is clear is that for far too long our political leadership in the West has failed to understand the danger, define it, and then develop specific strategies with which to defuse or defeat it. Past generations of American leaders have not suffered from the shortsightedness or negligence that characterizes our recent leaders.

Bold initiatives are needed on multiple fronts. We will supply here some proposals in each major category of problems:

FOREIGN RELATIONS

1) Forge new alliances with Russia, the European Union, India, China, and certain willing countries in Latin America to face down Islam.
2) Call an international conference, based on the model of the Potsdam Conference in 1945, to closely examine the teachings of Islam and to declare illegal certain of those teachings that imperil the safety of civil nations and their citizens.

3) Break up the power and unaccountability of the Organization of Islamic Conference in the United Nations. Member nations of the OIC must be expelled from the U.N. if they do not immediately implement the very Treaties of the U.N. that they agreed to observe as a condition of their admission into the U.N. Such treaties include the U.N. Charter and the Universal Declaration of Human Rights. Set up strict monitoring of their compliance with these treaties. Postpone any funding they presently receive under various U.N. programs, most of the money for which comes from Western countries. Ditch Resolution 16/18 of the Human Rights Council, and any similar proposed Resolution. Re-establish respect for what the United Nations is supposed to be under its founding documents, or leave it.

DOMESTIC

1) Pursue an immediate policy of energy self-sufficiency.
2) Establish a National Commission to carefully analyze the teachings of Islam, and to outlaw those teachings that violate our common laws. Use as a model the precedent cases of Reynolds (Mormons and polygamy) and Oregon v. Smith to properly redefine what can be taught in Islamic schools and mosques.
3) Review all existing laws to see which can be immediately applied to incarcerate seditious Muslim leaders, and closely monitor mosques and Islamic civic centers for seditious activity. Prosecute to the limits of the law those who violate our laws.

4) Establish a National Review Commission to carefully review the performance of Federal judges in enforcing our laws. Impeach and remove from office all those who refuse to strictly enforce our Constitution. Such refusal is a violation of the Oath of Office that they took.
5) Using Article 3, Section 2, 2nd paragraph of the U.S. Constitution, request the Congress to enact such "Exceptions" and "Regulations" on the jurisdiction of the U.S. Supreme Court as are required to restore domestic security. Let State courts exercise jurisdiction over all types of cases "excepted" from the jurisdiction of the Supreme Court.
6) End all Federal funding and assistance of any kind to "sanctuary cities."
7) Institute a program of close monitoring and inspection of mosques for illegal arms, literature, and illegal activity of any kind. If found in violation of our laws, close them down and permanently deport the imams responsible.
8) Trace and then systematically track the funding of all mosques and Islamic centers in the U.S. Permit no foreign funding of same.
9) Review all education manuals and introduce lessons in history that truthfully instruct our elementary and high school students on the true nature of Islam.Immediately end the refugee resettlement program and seek to deport those who have already arrived with temporary, reviewable status.
10) Revise immigration from Mexico and Latin America, with a view to more quickly admitting those who meet revised U.S criteria.

11) Declare the Muslim Brotherhood and all its affiliates terrorist organizations illegal. Enforce all applicable laws to arrest its principals and interrupt its funding.
12) Prosecute to the full extent of applicable law all the Unindicted Co-conspirators from the 2008 United States v. Holy Land Foundation case.
13) Immediately end NASA's Outreach to Muslim nations, instituted by President Obama. It has led to free transfer of space-related technology, which was paid for by the American taxpayer.

I know some will be shocked with the above list.

Nations need to defend themselves, especially when the enemy can be seen so clearly, once the fog of political correctness is lifted.

The United States has a right to defend itself, always within its laws. And now it must.

Some may think that adopting the above measures will lead to war. Pundits tell us that we must not, and cannot, declare war on an entire religion. But war has been declared on us already by that religion. That war manifests itself by both violent means and by "civilization jihad" means. Both are war. It is just some of our political leaders who do not want to admit it.

EPILOGUE

The world does not owe Islam anything.

There is no moral equivalence between Christianity and Islam. Christianity teaches love for our fellow human beings, and Islam teaches hate and cruelty to the "infidel." If some Christians have not properly observed the full teachings of love contained in Christianity over the ages that is not the fault of Christianity, it is their own fault. But Islam's teaching is consistent over the centuries and not subject to a different interpretation. In Islam's case, both its teaching and its interpretation, have been consistently violent. I repeat, therefore, there is no moral equivalence between Christianity and Islam.

If Islam seeks to convince us of its peaceful intentions, then it needs to be convincing with its actions. So far, many of its followers who amount to almost twenty-five percent of the world's population have abused the other seventy-five percent. This has got to stop, with convincing actions from within Islam. Reform, renunciation of conquest and of violence, and internal policing of inflammatory teachings in mosques and policing of would-be jihadis are now necessary.

All major faiths, including the Christian denominations, Judaism, Buddhism, and Hinduism have been capable of supplying convincing proof of their peaceful nature, except for Islam.

If the violence, abuse of "infidels," abuse of world institutions like the United Nations and its Charter and the world conquest aspirations of Islam are not corrected from within, then they will inevitably be corrected from without. History will repeat itself.

The increasing abuse and barbaric killing of Christians by the Global Islamic Movement will inevitably lead to retaliation. If imams continue to inflame young Muslims to violence, how long will those imams and their own families be safe from retribution? The question I pose here is simply based on observation of history and observation of human nature. Can we this time all avoid the black past of human history?

I repeat: can we live and let live?

Appendix 1

UTT THROWBACK THURSDAY ON 9/11 IN STEPS THE ENEMY

Thanks to Karl Rove and Grover Norquist, American President George W. Bush was able to turn to his left and right after the jihadi attacks on the United States on September 11, 2001 and find any of a number of Muslim Brotherhood/Hamas and/or Al Qaeda leaders (suit-wearing jihadis) to tell him how to fight the war.

Candidate Bush with Al Qaeda financier Abdurahman Alamoudi

Candidate Bush and Mrs. Bush with Hamas leader Sami al Arian in Florida (March 2000)

Republican strategist Grover Norquist and Muslim Brother Suhail Khan (who was working in the White House on 9/11). Khan is the son of Mahboob Khan, one of the most prolific Muslim Brotherhood leaders in North America in the 1960s to 1980s. Suhail also served as an assistant to two consecutive Secretaries of the Treasury with a Secret Clearance and continues to pass himself off as a "conservative Republican."

President Bush's visit to the Islamic Center of Washington (DC) after 9/11. On the right is Hamas Leader Nihad Awad (CAIR), and on the left is Khalid Saffuri (deputy to Al Qaeda operative Alamoudi).

Imam Muzammil Siddiqi, a senior MB leader in the U.S.—who is currently the Chairman of the Muslim Brotherhood's Fiqh Council of North America—at the memorial for 9/11 victims at the National Cathedral on 9/14/01

If you want to know how and why America lost the wars in Afghanistan and Iraq—despite President Bush's strong stand after 9/11 and our military's heroic efforts and great battlefield victories—it is because every time the President of the United States, the Secretary of State, military Generals and Admirals, leaders in our national security apparatus, and others turned for advice on how to proceed in the war or in any of our counterterrorism matters domestically, they were talking to the enemy.

And we still are.

AUTHOR BIOGRAPHY

Nicholas Papanicolaou was born in Athens, Greece. He holds a Bachelor's degree in Economics from Harvard University, a Master's degree from Colombia University School of Business, and a Doctorate degree in Theology from Phoenix University of Theology. He has enjoyed an active business career as a ship owner and former controlling shareholder and chairman of Aston Martin Lagonda Holding Ltd. U.K.

In 2002, he co-founded with Vladimir Yakunin of Russia and J.G. Kaupur of India the World Public Forum "Dialogue of Civilizations," an NGO registered in Vienna, Austria (www.wpfdc.com). The WPF brings together seven hundred delegates fro more than sixty different countries for four days every year on the island of Rhodes in Greece to openly discuss religious and cultural differences. WPF delegates have included the former Prime Ministers of India, Algeria, the Czech Republic, Austria, the former Presidents of Lithuania, Bangladesh, President Khatami of Iran, Slovakia, Armenia, Yemen, President Mahmoud Abbas of the Palestine Authority, and many other dignitaries, archbishops of the Orthodox church, Cardinals, Ayatollah Ali Taskhiri of Iran, Chief Rabbis and Chief Muftis.

Mr. Papanicolaou is the worldwide leader of the Knights of Saint John of Jerusalem Knights of Malta—The Ecumenical Order. This organization is an Order of Knighthood that is engaged in worldwide charity. Over the last few years, this Order has contributed more than $60 million in medicine and supplies to needy countries, including countries with large Muslim populations such as Pakistan, Indonesia, Liberia, and the Philippines. The Order speaks out when Christians are discriminated against because of their religion.

He has been honored with the grand cross of St. Andrew the First Called of Russia for his work on the dialogue of civilizations, the grand cross of Saint John of Jerusalem, the grand cross of the Imperial Spanish Order of Carlos V, the Royal Confraternity of Sao Teotonio of Portugal, the Stora Amaranther Order of Sweden, and the gold star of the National Rescue Service of the Ukraine for his humanitarian work.

The author with Cosmonaut Oleg A'tkov, Vladimir Yakunin, and Walther Schwimmer, President of the International Coordinating Committee of the World Public Forum "Dialogue of Civilizations" and former Secretary General of the Council of Europe.

The author with Patriarch Alexy II of Russia, Moscow 2006.

The author is the worldwide leader of the Sovereign Order of Saint John of Jerusalem (The Ecumenical Order), pictured here with his Honor Guard, in Toronto, Canada.

Investiture of the author as a Knight Grand Cross of the Swedish Order of the Amaranth, Stockholm, 2012.

Investiture of the author as a Knight Grand Cross of the Imperial Spanish Order of Carlos V, Spain, 2010.

World Public Forum "Dialogue of Civilizations", Rhodes, 2003.
Shown in front center are the three Co-Founders of the Forum: Vladimit Yakunin of Russia, J.C. Kapur of India, and Nicholas Papanicolaou of Greece.
Also shown: Prime Minister Gujral of India; President Adamkus of Lithuania; Professor Hamid Al-Rifaie (Co-President of the World Muslim Congress; and the Deputy Leader of Hezbollah.

SELECT ADDITIONAL READING

1. *DESTINY DISRUPTED: A HISTORY OF THE WORLD THROUGH ISLAMIC EYES*, by Tamim Ansary, 2010
2. *THEY MUST BE STOPPED*, by Brigitte Gabriel, St. Martin's Press, 2008
3. *DID MUHAMMAD EXIST?*, by Robert Spencer, ISI Books, 2012
4. *NO LIBERTY FOR LICENSE*, by Prof. David Lowenthal, Spence Publishing Company, 1997
5. *THE TIDES OF HISTORY*, by Jacques Pirenne, E.P. Dutton and Co., Inc., 1962
6. *MUSLIM MAFIA*, by David Gaubatz, WND Books, 2009
7. *THE EVERLASTING HATRED*, by Lindsey Hall, WND Books, 2011
8. *MUSLIM NEXT DOOR*, by Dr. Alfonse Javed, ANM Publishers, 2012
9. *THE RELIANCE OF THE TRAVELLER*, by Ahmad ibn Lulu ibn Al-Naqib, Amana Publications, 1991
10. *EMPIRES OF THE SEA*, by Roger Crowley, Random House Inc., 2008

11. *1453: THE HOLY WAR FOR CONSTANTINOPLE AND THE CLASH OF ISLAM AND THE WEST*, by Robert Crowley, 2006
12. *LOST TO THE WEST: THE FORGOTTEN BYZANTINE EMPIRE THAT RESCUED WESTERN CIVILIZATION*, by Lars Brownworth, 2010.
13. *THE PEDAGOGY OF ARAB GOVERNANCE,* by Dr. Saleh S. Al-Jallad, published by Mirrors For Princes, 2015

Made in the USA
Middletown, DE
18 February 2025

71197025R00144